WHAT MOTIVATES GETTING THINGS DONE

WHAT MOTIVATES GETTING THINGS DONE

Procrastination, Emotions, and Success

Mary Lamia

ROWMAN & LITTLEFIELD
Lanham • Boulder • New York • London

Published by Rowman & Littlefield
A wholly owned subsidiary of The Rowman & Littlefield Publishing Group,
Inc.
4501 Forbes Boulevard, Suite 200, Lanham, Maryland 20706
www.rowman.com

Unit A, Whitacre Mews, 26-34 Stannary Street, London SE11 4AB

British Library Cataloguing in Publication Information Available

Library of Congress Cataloging-in-Publication Data Is Available

ISBN 978-1-4422-0381-5 (cloth: alk. paper)
ISBN 978-1-4422-0382-2 (electronic)

♾ ™ The paper used in this publication meets the minimum requirements of
American National Standard for Information Sciences Permanence of Paper
for Printed Library Materials, ANSI/NISO Z39.48-1992.

Printed in the United States of America

CONTENTS

ACKNOWLEDGMENTS

Wisdom, information, and advice were offered by colleagues, friends, and family members throughout versions of the manuscript for this book. Much appreciation goes to Marilyn Krieger; Scott Hughes; William McCown; Gary David; Deborah Malmud; Linda McCarter; Jeanne Bergin; and Ann, Julian, David, and Frederick Parris. Jason Strauss and his assistants at the Wright Institute library helped with difficult-to-find resources for this book, and I am grateful for their time and efforts. Special appreciation goes to Suzanne Staszak-Silva for her confidence in my work.

I am truly indebted to numerous people who informed my understanding of what motivates them to get things done either ahead of schedule or at the deadline. Since stigma often accompanies procrastination, I hold in high regard all of the deadline-driven procrastinators who felt safe enough to be interviewed or to complete questionnaires that helped me understand what motivates their style of task completion. Not everyone who informed this work was successful at getting things done. Thus, I also want to express my admiration and hope for those who let me into their emotional lives in ways that provided insight as to why some people fail and, instead, attribute it to procrastinating.

INTRODUCTION

What motivates successful people to get things done? Maybe you assume their motivation is fueled by imagining a future reward for their efforts, including the joyful feeling of pride. However, a marvel of evolution is that humans are not solely motivated by positive emotions. They are also motivated, and even driven to achieve, by negative emotions—a primary, powerful, and often misunderstood source of motivation. How does that work?

Essentially, people are motivated to do something based on their desire to turn on positive emotions or to turn off negative emotions.[1] It's just a fundamental principle about how we function emotionally. Labeling emotions as positive or negative has little to do with their value but instead involves how they motivate us through the ways they make us feel. Negative emotions, such as distress, fear, anger, disgust, and shame, motivate us to do something to avoid experiencing them, or they urge us to behave in ways that will relieve their effects. There is no doubt that negative emotions, along with positive ones, significantly influence our lives by silently directing the decisions we make and motivating us to get things done. Moreover, how we learn from dealing with core emotions, to a great extent, makes us who we become.

High achievers are motivated by their emotions to put effort into their work and never miss a deadline, although some may complete a task minutes before the cutoff point. In fact, while many successful people can't resist the urge to do things right away, countless others put things off until a deadline beckons them. The different timing of procrastinators and nonprocrastinators to complete tasks has to do with *when* their emotions are activated and *what* activates them. Through exploring the emotional lives of people who are successful in their endeavors—both deadline-driven procrastinators and task-driven nonprocrastinators alike—this book explains how the human motivational system works, why people respond to it differently, and how to use it to your advantage. In these pages you will discover the impact of your emotional life on your style of doing, along with your way of being in the world. You'll understand why you *should* fear failure, the many ways in which anxiety *is* your friend, and how *negative emotions* can drive the pursuit of excellence.

Numerous studies have investigated procrastination behavior, often seeking to find some underlying pathology or undesirable characteristic that leads people to delay.[2] The possible "causes" of procrastination under investigation are wide ranging, and a prevailing objective of these studies has to do with the search for successful interventions to reduce the frequency of procrastination in those who do it. As a result, educators, clinicians, college counselors, and authors of self-help books have attempted to turn procrastinators into people who complete tasks well in advance of a deadline. However, they have been ineffective in their mission.[3] Estimates of procrastination among college students range from 70 to 95 percent, and obviously, they're not all failing.[4] Perhaps the actual explanation for why many procrastinators don't change is they have no reason to alter their approach: it effectively works for them. Nevertheless, sometimes successful people who procrastinate experience shame or guilt about their task-completion style, or the judgment of others leads them to feel that way, even though they are not inclined to change their style of doing things.[5]

I could not write a book about the motivation to get things done without recognizing my readers will differ in what motivates their interest. Surely, some sections or chapters will captivate your interest more than others. The emotion of interest is one of the helpful innate tools that we have at our disposal to motivate task completion, yet our experiences lead us to differ in terms of what activates it. Therefore, I have written the book so that, if you prefer, you can skip around to sections that greater engage your attention or skip over sections that do not interest you. In some of the chapters I am prominently wearing my professorial hat, in others I use my voice as a clinician, and on occasion

I am simply being human. In any case, I hope to resonate with you emotionally. Some people are excited by theory or details, whereas others are not. Given those differences, you will find endnotes for most of the chapters that include research and speculations for readers who are inclined to seek further information.

The first chapter provides an overview of what is covered in the book, including an evident example of a deadline-driven procrastinator, a task-driven nonprocrastinator, and a couple in the midst of attempting to navigate their divergent styles of getting things done. Chapter 2 describes some of the unique characteristics of deadline-driven procrastinators and task-driven nonprocrastinators. Some of the characteristics of procrastinators and nonprocrastinators are contrary to commonsense expectations! You may find yourself solidly identifying with the behavioral descriptions of a particular style. However, if you determine you do not have a dominant task-completion style, much like being ambidextrous, you may want to consider the elements of each style that may work best for you. Chapter 3 was written with the goal in mind of conveying what emotions are and how they operate. Learning just a little about the underpinnings of motivation can help you make use of the system that guides you.

If you are interested in understanding why you become anxious around tasks to complete, you'll learn in Chapter 4 why anxiety can be a great friend—perhaps even a personal coach—when it comes to getting things done. If you are aware of fearing failure when something must get done, that information will be found in Chapter 5. There, you will discover why you *should* fear failure, more specifically, how shame anxiety can be highly motivating. However, if you are most interested in what drives people to achieve and why successful people tend to be perfectionists, then you will be drawn to Chapter 6, where you will discover what motivates the pursuit of excellence.

Perhaps you are most interested in problems that exist in your relationship with someone who has an approach to tasks that differs from yours. Then again, maybe you just want to deal with your annoyance about the way other people do things. Since navigating through conflict and learning from differences is important in all relationships, the information provided in Chapter 7 may positively alter your interactions with others where motivational style differences can otherwise become a source of conflict. Chapter 8 provides some specific ways in which you can optimize your motivational style, and they are summarized in the troubleshooting guide found in Chapter 9. The final chapter has to do with the influence of emotions in general as you look back on your experiences and move forward.

The opinions in this book are based on surveys and interviews I conducted with professionally successful people who procrastinate and those who do not. Further speculations and conclusions are drawn from my nearly four decades of practice as a clinical psychologist and psychoanalyst, as well as from my work as a professor in a clinical psychology doctoral program. In these various contexts, many people have described what motivates how they get things done.

Lastly, in the interest of full disclosure, I am not a procrastinator. Therefore, I do not have a stake in vindicating procrastinators or exposing the limitations of those who complete tasks ahead of schedule, although such themes are present in the book. Primarily, I hope to convey something far more important: emotions are fascinating to explore in every aspect of human behavior. How they motivate the completion of tasks in different ways is no exception. It's time to make the most of the motivational system that evolved to help us get things done.

Chapter 1

WHAT MOTIVATES GETTING THINGS DONE

An Overview

Some people put things off until a deadline looms, and others seem compelled to complete tasks immediately. Does procrastination interfere with success? Definitely not. Those who wait to complete tasks are just as likely to be successful as people who complete tasks ahead of time. Procrastination should not be linked with failure just as early action should not be tied to success.

The primary source of motivation to complete tasks, whether or not you procrastinate, isn't a big secret: emotions are intrinsic to all human motivation. Perhaps you've assumed you are not motivated by your emotions but, instead, only by what you think—your cognitions—when it comes to tackling a major project or even a mundane task. However, you cannot think yourself into being motivated to do something without the help of emotion. In Chapter 3, we delve more deeply into the subject of the role of emotion in motivation. For now let's consider the notion, believed by many, that people are motivated by positive thoughts, such as anticipating a sense of pride when a task has been completed.

The image of experiencing future pride is not only cognitive; thoughts can instantaneously, but not necessarily consciously, access our internal warehouse of emotional memories where joyful pleasure associated with our efforts was previously felt. These emotional memories can involve anything, from the long-forgotten joy mirrored in the face of caregivers celebrating our first steps to recently felt enjoyment about an accomplishment. Thus, in response to imagery, emotional memories activate present feeling reminders that can fuel our motivation to accomplish something. As such, many people experience an "addiction" to the positive feeling that is stimulated by accomplishment, and their present efforts are highly motivated by emotional memories of positive feelings around success. A stark contrast is found in people who have repeatedly failed, for example, those who have low motivation that accompanies a significant depression. They may have difficulty accessing memories of excitement or joy. Instead, their pessimistic thoughts around the possibility of their efforts leading to a successful outcome, along with their emotional memories of failure, may activate fear, distress, or shame. It is no wonder that people with a history of failure might cope with their feelings around a present challenge by withdrawing effort or avoiding any engagement with a task. Their warehouse of memories may lead them to anticipate the familiar negative emotions associated with defeat.

A core process in the human brain coordinates feeling with thinking. Biologically based emotions are the primary motivational component of that process—they are the engine of motivation. We are not always consciously aware of the emotional signals our brains send to our bodies that create a sense of urgency, direct our attention, and produce thoughts and images influencing our decisions. Thoughts that accompany emotions give meaning to what we feel and enable us to minimize, amplify, act on, or ignore the message an emotion is attempting to convey. In some ways, our emotions are like the dinging sound of a notification that appears on a computer screen. These messages garner our attention, and our thoughts enable us to determine their meaning and make a decision regarding whether we should attend to them.

When an emotion is activated, it is filtered through your personal history and culture, linking with all of your memories when a similar emotion was triggered. This complex process produces the distinctive ways we experience and express an emotion and makes for interesting differences among people, including the uniqueness of their personalities. Thus, the ability for some people to be motivated to attend immediately to a task, whereas others delay with impunity, is to a large extent, a result of the interaction of their biology and personal history.

A simple example will illustrate how emotions work alongside the thoughts that accompany them. Imagine getting into your car while holding a café mocha you have just purchased. You inadvertently squeeze the cup, the top pops off, and the coffee spills all over the car seat. You may experience a variety of emotions at that moment, and certainly you will feel some combination of startle and distress. Distress alone can motivate you to clean up the mess, but likely in such situations, startle and distress will blend with anger, which can lead you to curse in response to the spill and be agitated as you wipe it up. However, motivation to clean up the mess will also result if your brain triggers both distress and fear—a combination we often refer to as "anxiety," which may be accompanied by the thought that you will stain your clothes if you sit down on any smudge that is left from the mocha. Even greater motivation to clean up the mess and do it well will result if your brain adds shame to fear and distress, which may arise with the thought of sitting on a remaining chocolate smudge, staining your pants, and someone thinking you had an "accident."

At an emotional level, the combination of fear, distress, and shame produces *shame anxiety*—anticipating the possibility of experiencing shame. When fear, distress, and shame arise together, the thoughts that accompany this combination of emotions commonly lead people to conclude they "fear failure." The emotions behind a fear of failure and how people effectively use them to get things done are discussed in Chapter 5.

Just to further the amazing possibilities emotions create, what do you imagine feeling if your brain activates both negative and positive emotions, such as distress and fear, along with excitement? Generally, in terms of getting things done, this combination is what people describe as a sense of "flow" or "being in the zone." However, it's unlikely those emotions will be activated together when you spill a café mocha on the seat of your car. If you have someone with you who responds with surprise, he or she may find the mishap very amusing—but probably will not expose what he or she feels until later, when, hopefully, you can laugh together. The example of what motivates cleaning up a spilled café mocha may not have convinced you that emotions motivate behavior; however, I count on persuading you before you are halfway through this book.

Regardless of whether a person procrastinates, certain situations, such as the above scenario, will activate an emotional response that creates an urgency to take action. Nonetheless, the different timing of procrastinators and nonprocrastinators to complete tasks has to do with *when* their emotions are activated and *what* activates them. Procrastinators who consistently complete tasks on time—even if they do so at the last moment—are motivated by emotions that are activated when a deadline is imminent. They are *deadline driven*. In this book, I often refer to individuals who intentionally delay task completion as deadline driven in an attempt to remove negative judgment about delay and to recognize a valid motivational style. Nonetheless, there are many times in citing literature and using common vernacular that I use the word "procrastinator" or a derivative of the word. Therefore, I define procrastinators as *people who are primarily motivated to complete tasks when their emotions are activated by an imminent deadline. They are deadline driven.* The formal definition of procrastination is "to put off intentionally the doing of something that should be done."[1] This definition does not necessarily imply that tasks are not completed successfully and on time. Indeed, purposely delaying an intended course of action, a common understanding of procrastination in the research literature, is not synonymous with insufficient action or a failure to act. I'll say more about this in Chapter 2.

In contrast to procrastinators, *task-driven* people (nonprocrastinators) faced with uncompleted tasks are compelled to take action right away. Motivated by their emotions to complete a task ahead of schedule and put it behind them, those who are successful attend to the quality of their work prior to scratching the task off their list. Thus, procrastinators are motivated by emotions that are activated by deadlines, and task-driven people are motivated by emotions that are triggered by the task itself. In the case of a situation such as a spilled café mocha, the task and the deadline coincide. How people with these different task-completion styles effectively employ the emotions that motivate them is explained in this book.

Motivational styles generally develop at a young age, and many people can link their particular style to memories of completing school assignments or everyday tasks. Early response patterns to emotion—such as when emotion was activated that motivated you to complete your homework or make your bed—continue to influence how you tend to get things done throughout your life. You might assume you did these things just because you were *supposed* to do them. Although you may not have been aware of feeling a particular emotion but instead only having thoughts, such as "I should make my bed," I can assure you that emotion was present motivating you to do it. These early life experiences, at some point, solidify into characteristic emotional responses to tasks and lead to a particular style of getting things done. Here, we can recognize the importance of not forming value judgments about a particular style because, like our taste for certain foods, task completion styles develop from the emotions we experience early in life.

Since our biologically based core emotions, when activated, are instantaneously filtered through our personal history, culture, and implicit memories where that emotion was previously activated, we are bound to be "messed up" in some of the ways we interpret our emotional lives. An example has to do with people who consistently fail to get things done. When delay is involved and a deadline passes, failure is not simply a result of procrastinating. Usually, an entirely separate emotional issue or some other obstacle has interfered with the person's completing his or her work. Unlike successful deadline-driven people, the so-called procrastinators who fail are not motivated by their emotional responses when a deadline looms. Rather, their emotional responses further disable them. When the deadline passes they blame their failure on procrastinating rather than explore what's really going on. Many therapists, teachers, family members, and self-help books also view failure as having to do with procrastinating rather than recognize the more complex emotional issues impeding an individual's success.

Emotional issues may also interfere with the success of nonprocrastinators. These issues are often hidden because, while nonprocrastinators do complete their work, the quality of what is produced may be poor. Cognitively, they may value getting things done or comply with instructions to complete a task, yet other issues likely interfere with the emotions that can motivate efforts to do their best work. In addition, people who dislike leaving tasks unfinished experience an urgency to seek relief by getting things done. Some task-driven people feel as though their attention to tasks is at the expense of relaxing or engaging in enjoyable activities.

In everyday interactions we are often unaware of another person's task-completion style unless we live or work with him or her. That said,

I'll now introduce you to Judith and Ryan, who may appear as extreme illustrations of task-driven and deadline-driven individuals, respectively. If you met either of them at a dinner party or professional event, and even if you became somewhat familiar with them, chances are you would be unaware of how they operate emotionally when it comes to getting things done; however, once you've read this book you will recognize the subtle characteristics of each style. Given the conflicts that result when people clash because of their different motivational styles, you will increase your understanding of what makes people tick, and you may be better able to work or live with others who have such differences.

First let's meet task-driven Judith, a high-level executive in sports advertising who is far from being a procrastinator. Judith, having come from an impoverished background and "saved" by a college scholarship to play basketball, views her successful career as a perfect match, as well as a blessing. Each day as she enters the office, Judith becomes anxious. Keep in mind that the actual basis of Judith's anxiety is unknown. The thoughts that arise with the sensations she feels provide an assumed source for her that justifies why she is anxious. For Judith, the thoughts that account for her anxiety have to do with what she needs to get done each day. So the first thing she does is list her pending work-related tasks on a pad of paper, but in addition and on the same list, she includes bills to pay, travel plans, appointments, and matters regarding her partner and children. She recognizes that some of those tasks can wait, but unfinished tasks are distressing to her. She also feels uncomfortable tension when she has to keep something in mind for another day rather than write it on the day's to-do list and scratch it off when it's done. Judith's "fear of forgetting" constantly reminds her of what remains uncompleted. The list helps her in that regard. When completing one of the tasks on her list depends on the action of another person, Judith becomes very agitated if she has to wait longer than she deems reasonable, especially because the delay interferes with her anticipated relief in getting the task off her list.

Ordinarily, Judith diligently and methodically proceeds through her list, crossing off each to-do item she completes. However, the fact that the item still exists on the list, even though it is crossed out, distracts and irritates her as though it remains as something to do. Therefore, Judith rewrites the list on the next sheet of paper and eliminates the completed task. She then tears off the old list from the pad, crumples it up, and with a sense of relief from her anxiety, tosses the ball of paper into the recycling container. Along with the relief from the negative emotion, Judith executes the toss in such a manner as to awaken pleasurable memories of her college basketball days. Since playing basketball was significant in her life, every toss is enjoyable, and many are even exciting. Judith's goal, challenging at times, is to get through a day with all the items crossed off and all her various sheets of crumpled paper successfully lobbed into the "basket," leaving only a blank sheet on top of her desk to greet her the following morning. On the days she meets the challenge she experiences a joyful sense of accomplishment.

Every so often Judith has an urgency to complete a particular task immediately but also feels daunted in tackling. In such situations she begins to daydream, for example, about the tornado warnings in her college town that had everyone scrambling into the shelters. She muses that some natural disaster might happen that would take her away from the urgency she feels to complete the dreaded task. As her dread becomes greater and she seeks relief from what she feels, she begins working on the task.

Rarely do we question why some people are compelled to complete tasks right away; however, if you live or work with someone who cannot put tasks aside until later you may have wondered whether his or her behavior reflects a pathological condition, even though it may not. Being task driven, Judith has found a productive way to utilize the negative emotions she experiences when a task is pending: she successfully gets things done. Conversely, some task-driven people may become self-destructive in their efforts to avoid anxiety or seek relief from how it feels. Rather than effectively use their anxiety, like Judith does, they might instead medicate it with legal or illegal substances. Disregarding the accuracy of their work, people who are not effective in using their negative emotions might hurriedly attend to something just to get it behind them. In other instances, they might handle the anxiety about forgetting or the shame of failing by ignoring the need for further consideration or collaboration just to complete a task early.

Now, meet deadline-driven Ryan, a marketing consultant who claims he procrastinates "like a psycho." Ryan intensely worries when a particular project is pending and he has not tangibly started to work on it. In one situation the deadline for a project was in a week. He had taken on the project two months before and since that time had been mulling it over in his mind and generally developing a strategy to tackle it. However, he was not motivated to directly attend to it.

Ryan does not have the interest, energy, or drive to begin an important project unless there is significant tension in terms of time. As tension builds, his energy becomes more intense, along with a change in what distracts him: he is compelled to do *something* and notices many things that need to be done, aside from the project. During such times he feels guilty and blames himself for being diverted by all of the distracting tasks that seem to demand attention. He spotlessly cleans his house, spends time exercising, and thoroughly researches wilderness biking expeditions. Meanwhile, images of the various pieces of the project begin to appear in his consciousness.

Predictably, as the deadline draws closer, Ryan wonders whether he should request an extension—a typical thought he has at such times—although he is well aware that such a request would lead him to lose face. Further, the relief he would experience from an extension would be short-lived because, eventually, he would be in the same situation. During such times he finds himself engaged in conversations with colleagues, relatives, and anyone else who will listen about the stress of his career and alternate paths he considers (but really isn't interested in pursuing). People who are close to him seem to take on his concerns, worry that he will fail, and suggest various exit strategies. Eventually, when the deadline is looming, Ryan experiences highly uncomfortable shame anxiety, which leads him to fear that he will fail, yet it thrusts him into gear. At that point, nothing can interfere with his intense focus on the project. Although the stress of completing a task is concentrated near a deadline, Ryan retrospectively refers to it as "good stress," noting he is constantly amazed at how precisely and successfully he always completes projects on time.

If you put yourself in the shoes of Ryan's family members, friends, or colleagues who listen to his angst before tackling a project, you might suggest various ways he could manage what he feels, including finding a new career. You might think of him as a stress case and suggest he should have started earlier, should see a therapist, or might benefit from taking medication. His partner, who has become familiar with Ryan's way of doing things, simply listens and reassures him that he always gets things done. Even so, once he gets down to work on a project, his partner imagines the space around Ryan as being like the eye of a hurricane, and she resists interrupting him.

Understanding how emotions motivate different task-completion approaches is also important in business relationships and intimate partnerships and for people who work in teams. Procrastinators want people around them to trust they will complete tasks before the deadline, yet those who finish things ahead of time wish the procrastinators in their lives would notice all the tasks that need to be done and participate in working on them—now, rather than later. People with different task-completion styles who live together seem to have a particularly hard time when a situation or circumstance reveals their differences and they do not understand the emotions that motivate each other's behavior.

In this regard, I introduce you to Kelly and Daniel, who described an example—another extreme illustration—that occurred when they were in their car and headed for the airport. They had driven only three blocks when task-driven Kelly insisted that Daniel, her deadline-driven husband, turn the car around and drive back to the house because she had not put cleaning tablets into the toilets. Daniel argued that it could wait. Kelly explained that she had intended to try out new nontoxic cleaning tablets while they were away; however, since he had gone out the door early and started the car, she had felt rushed and had forgotten. In a final effort to get Daniel to turn the car around and go back to the house, Kelly told him since he procrastinates and never does his share of bathroom cleaning she was just trying to be efficient and make it possible for herself to relax while on vacation. Angry and wanting to avoid further blame, Daniel reluctantly made a U-turn and headed back. Subsequently, the ride to the airport was unpleasant; nevertheless, Daniel was relieved that they still arrived early, and Kelly was thankful that she had completed everything on her to-do list.

As an aside, although it may seem counterintuitive, many deadline-driven procrastinators, like Daniel, prefer to arrive early. Just because they are motivated by deadlines does not translate into being late or barely on time. Contrarily, many task-driven people, like Kelly, do not prefer an extra-early arrival and view it as a misuse of time. In addition, an erroneous assumption is often made that people who self-identify as procrastinators are not interested in doing their share of housework. In subsequent chapters I'll address these issues and explain why, based on the motivation provided by emotion, such generalizations are not applicable. For the moment, please just believe me.

Now, let's take a look at some of the unique characteristics of deadline-driven procrastinators and task-driven nonprocrastinators. Their differences and similarities will serve as a framework for later chapters when we explore exactly how emotions play a significant role in what motivates people.

Chapter 2

DEADLINES, DELIBERATION, AND DISTRACTION

As a couple Melissa and Sam were invited to participate in a ceremony for which they had three months to prepare. Melissa was asked to recite a poem, and Sam was asked to give the opening speech. Consistent with her task-driven style, Melissa began memorizing the poem right away. Typical of task-driven people, she likes to prepare in advance—just in case something happens. The possible interference could be anything because, as she put it, you never know what could stand in the way of getting something done. Sam accommodated Melissa's requests to be her practice audience; however, eventually he limited how much time he'd spend doing it.

Intermittently, and with a hint of agitation in her voice, Melissa asked Sam whether he had prepared his part. As a procrastinator, Sam put off tangibly working on the talk, leaving it to "marinate" in his head. "During that time," he clarified, "I worked on it at a subconscious level—in my yoga class, walking, sleeping. At some point, much like a solution or steps to a solution, the content of the talk started to come together."

Expressing her annoyance with Sam in similar circumstances, Melissa remarked, "He makes me nuts when he waits. I try to let it go and let him do his thing, but I don't get why he does this last-minute stuff." Sam contends that Melissa just worries too much about when he will get things done.

The evening prior to the ceremony Sam created an outline of his talk. According to Melissa it was after 11:00 p.m., they were in the hotel room, and she was in bed peering past the sheets at Sam's notes scattered across the covers. In the morning, Melissa went for a walk, knowing she would have a hard time being in the room while Sam was finishing his talk. When he is in that mode, she explained, he doesn't answer her questions and sometimes doesn't even seem to hear her speak. She knew he'd be a different person when she returned, that is, if he was finished. Sam wrote out his talk while Melissa was on her walk. "I knew exactly what I wanted to say," he explained. "On one level, it may be called procrastination, but I think it is a way to more fully use the brainpower I have."

You may identify more with Sam's deadline-driven approach, with Melissa's task-driven approach, or possibly with both styles of task completion. What they have in common is an important attribute of professionally successful people: they effectively meet deadlines and their work reflects their best efforts.[1] In later chapters we'll explore exactly what motivates them. For now, let's take a look at how they differ in terms of deadlines, deliberating about tasks, and distractibility as background for subsequent chapters that delve into how the human motivational system works and why people respond to it differently. Moreover, if you live or work with someone whose motivational style differs from yours, any annoyance or frustration you felt about his or her unique style of getting things done may have interfered with your objectivity about a particular approach. This chapter will help familiarize you with how deadline-driven and task-driven people function externally before we find out how emotions determine their behavior.

MEETING DEADLINES

Generally, most people identify as being or not being a procrastinator.[2] Others consider themselves as not having a specific style of task completion, or they view their motivational style as context dependent: in some situations, they delay but at other times they do not. Procrastinators commonly hesitate to expose their style, not wanting to admit their inclination to wait until a deadline is near before completing a task.

Often, their secrecy is born out of a history of criticism from others or the general stigma surrounding procrastination.

Notwithstanding their preference to wait until the deadline is near, under certain circumstances procrastinators are motivated to complete tasks early. For instance, they might choose to complete a task right away if interpersonal conflict will result from delay. In this case, the motive has to do with conflict avoidance rather than a true versatility with both styles. Resentment as well as relief can follow this kind of acquiescence. A deadline-driven executive explained that certain tasks led him to think about the possibility of undesirable consequences and feelings if he didn't get them done immediately. Thus, wanting to avoid a negative outcome created some urgency. As he put it, "I initially prioritize tasks as they arise. High-priority tasks are those set by my wife, safety or health issues, and money—the longer I wait the more it costs. These tasks get done quickly given how I will feel if I don't do them."

Task-driven people, in contrast to procrastinators, are prideful about doing . . . and doing . . . and doing. They assume they do more than the procrastinators around them. Almost always they do whatever beckons them, and they finish well before a deadline. Actually, they're always doing things that don't even have a deadline, although they may feel as though the deadline is now.

Most successful people, regardless of their preferred approach to tasks, are not rigidly bound to a specific way of getting things done—task-driven people are able to delay, and procrastinators can do things ahead of time. Throughout the book I discuss some of the tricks they use to motivate themselves differently when they believe it is necessary to change their preferred approach. However, keep in mind that, for the most part, they have a natural default setting either to procrastinate or to attend immediately to tasks. Waiting until a deadline is near is not optimal for task-driven people in terms of concentration and decision making. So they delay only if it is necessary or for some other extraneous reason (e.g., other responsibilities prevent them from attending to the task as early as they would like). They generally don't miss deadlines, because they like to complete tasks as soon as possible. This may sound like a desirable quality, but it has its own drawbacks, which you'll come to recognize as you read through this book.

One drawback has to do with having a goal of getting something done over and above the quality of the work. However, this is not a drawback for task-driven people who focus on work quality because they know they will have time to make revisions. In written work, for example, they may go through many drafts before they have a finished product, usually well before a deadline. Another drawback in finishing something early is the potential that the individual will take a look at it again later, after it has already been submitted. Successful task-driven people are adept at self-supervision and can always find a way to improve on what they have done. Yet if they turn in written work early, they may be mortified upon rereading the document and seeing mistakes or places where improvement could have been made. So it wouldn't be unusual for a task-driven person to e-mail something to you and then send a modified version he or she wants you to read instead. In contrast, procrastinators typically complete a written project in one draft: the final draft. The earlier versions of their work are in their heads, and as such, the quality of their work doesn't suffer.

Accomplished people worry about uncompleted tasks. However, the more they consider themselves to be procrastinators, the less bothered they are by something not finished until a deadline is in sight. If you identify with task-driven Melissa, you may not be able to fathom why Sam, her deadline-driven partner, does not have her same sense of urgency to prepare his part for the ceremony. But if you are a procrastinator, you may be more apt to see why someone like Sam would be puzzled by Melissa's pressing need to get ready in advance.

Generally, early action is not questioned, but delay has always been scrutinized. For the most part, but not completely, Melissa assumed Sam would finish what he had to do prior to the ceremony because that's his pattern. Yet many task-driven people who are partnered with a procrastinator have doubts about whether something will get done in time, regardless of repeated exposure to their partner's process. Incomplete tasks seem to annoy task-driven people, even when these tasks are the responsibility of their partner. Thus, they may be inclined to get a little pushy about things long before the deadline.

As well, procrastination researchers doubt the efficacy of deadline-driven people. Few have studied the differences between procrastinators who never fail at task completion and those who habitually miss deadlines. Toward this end, a study by Angela Chu from Columbia

University and Jin Choi from McGill University distinguished between *active* and *passive* procrastinators.[3] *Active* procrastinators are motivated by last-minute time pressure and the feeling of being challenged. Although active procrastinators deliberately suspend their actions and may focus their attention on other tasks, they are able to act on decisions in a timely manner. In contrast, *passive* procrastinators have weak self-efficacy beliefs (low confidence in their ability to reach goals or complete tasks) and delay because they are unable to make decisions or act on them quickly. Passive procrastinators eventually give up or fail to complete tasks. The study by Chu and Choi illustrates the importance in procrastination research of separating the subset of the population who habitually fail to meet deadlines from those individuals whose style is simply deadline driven.

Even when procrastinators consistently meet deadlines, they are assumed to have pathological traits or conditions that account for the delay. In this regard, I want to let you know about a study that pertains specifically to deadlines. The study in question involved how well college students estimate the amount of time they needed to get something done.[4] The assumption of the researchers was that procrastinators, more than nonprocrastinators, would tend to underestimate the amount of time required to complete a task. Thus, they predicted that procrastinators would be prone to "planning fallacy." Unexpectedly, the researchers found procrastinators to be as competent as nonprocrastinators in matters pertaining to time estimation and at attaining the study goals they predicted. The investigators explained that when a deadline is absolute, such as an exam date set by a professor, both nonprocrastinators and procrastinators alike set realistic study plans and met them. However, the researchers speculated that when the prediction of a deadline is more flexible, such as predicting the completion date of a thesis, procrastinators would fall short. However, this is not the case. When deadlines are not absolute or clearly defined, how then do procrastinators successfully meet them?

Procrastinators describe various ways in which they create absolute deadlines when the cutoff point is not clearly defined or when it is best to complete a task early. A deadline can be constructed by interjecting other tasks that require attention, thereby limiting available future time. If a report must be completed sometime within a three-week period, for example, but business travel is planned for two of those weeks, the deadline for the proposal would need to be set to within the remaining week. One successful strategy they employ is to use a to-do list that they resolve to get through by the end of the day. This strategy narrows the time available to complete certain tasks. A daily to-do list also allows time to do other things until the end-of-the-day deadline approaches. Some procrastinators give themselves a specified amount of time, such as an hour, to work on something. As mentioned earlier by the deadline-driven executive, financial considerations are also effective for establishing an absolute deadline. This is especially so for those whose income is based on commission or project completion. An absolute deadline may also be determined by interpersonal concerns, such as the possibility of incurring the disappointment or disapproval of a colleague or partner. In some circumstances, procrastinators simply ask a partner or manager for an absolute deadline when it is indeterminate.

A high-achieving student who self-identifies as a procrastinator illustrated her proficiency at establishing absolute deadlines. Motivated to get through her doctoral program with minimal cost (determined by time), she created an absolute deadline for each step and substep involved in writing her dissertation. Her first step, for example, involved writing a prospectus that required approval before proceeding. She scheduled consultation meetings with a professor who potentially could serve on her dissertation committee, thereby creating an absolute deadline (the meeting time) for the completion of a specific substep (an outline of her prospectus) in the process. At various points she would notify the professor that she would be sending certain content on a specific date. She met all of her self-imposed deadlines.

Deadline Extension and Escape Fantasies

When deadlines are flexible or draw near, procrastinators often engage in deadline-extension fantasies. However, those who are successful in their ventures recognize these extension fantasies as their mind's way of trying to find a solution for their discomfort. They don't take seriously the possibility of extending the deadline, and their imagined humiliation about asking for more time also limits them. Instead, they give it up, and as a solution they will take action regarding the task at hand. Those who are proficient have learned that an extension is just another deadline at which time they would likely muse about yet another extension, such as in the case of Ryan in Chapter 1. Unfortunately, some people repeatedly make extension fantasies a reality, and as a result these people are more likely to fail. They may also blame their failure on procrastinating rather than explore what's really going on within them.

Task-driven people have a counterpart to the procrastinator's extension fantasies. When they are up against a task that seems daunting, they have fantasies of escape. They might imagine that a natural disaster, a weather-related obstacle, or a physical ailment might get them out of what they have to do. If only it would happen. Yet eventually they give up their fantasies of fate or illness helping them escape the situation, and they get to work.

Timeliness and Deadlines

Some people assume that procrastinators would arrive late or barely make it on time for everything—unless you are one of them and know better. Timeliness, such as getting to appointments on time or making a flight, is in fact, not associated with procrastination. First of all, getting something done at or just before a deadline does not constitute being late. Even so, those who delay are considered late when judged by the temporal standards of task-driven early birds. Missing a deadline defines being late. In any case, the behavior people exhibit around task deadlines is curiously transformed in other situations.

Consider air travel as an example. Air travel is an arena wherein timeliness is important because deadlines are absolute. Missing a flight or barely making it constitutes lateness. Logic tells us that deadline-driven procrastinators would likely arrive later for a flight than their task-driven counterparts; yet logic can be wrong. In fact, many, if not most, self-identified procrastinators claim they prefer to arrive early to the airport so they can relax, read, think, or watch people. In this scenario, procrastinators may seem capable of doing nothing when actually they are doing something, even if that something is just hanging out. In contrast, task-driven people experience early arrival for a flight as inefficient—it's a waste of time. Rather than wait and do nothing, they imagine all the things they could be getting done. There are some variations on this theme, and the issue becomes more complex than just whether people with a particular motivational style arrive early or late for a flight; for example, task-driven people might arrive early for a flight to continue to work on a project they have taken with them, whereas procrastinators may view a flight as a deadline that will prompt them to complete unfinished tasks prior to leaving for the airport. As a result, they may not arrive early.

For different reasons then, both task-driven people and deadline-driven procrastinators may get things done minutes before leaving their homes or offices to go somewhere. Task-driven people are often later than they would like to be or rushed to arrive somewhere on time because they become distracted by random tasks that seem to have an immediate calling. Getting out the door is difficult because there's always something they can do before leaving the house and usually it's many things. They perceive themselves as efficient, and if there is a minute, they'll make use of it. Procrastinators may also have a hard time getting out the door if they use the deadline to be somewhere else as a deadline for finishing a particular task or activity. Thus, this may result in a last-minute flurry of getting things done.

Task-Driven and Deadline-Driven Remorse

Both deadline-driven and task-driven people often have regret about how they do things. This regret occurs because, in general, successful people evaluate and reevaluate themselves. Looking back, procrastinators wonder, for example, whether they could have performed even better if they had given more time to a task, whether what they did in the meantime was valuable, or whether their deadline stress was worth the effort. A deadline-driven attorney said, "When it is the ninth hour, I am able to laser focus and create something really great, but then I always beat myself up about it, that maybe it could have been even better than great." Task-driven people often question their decisions, wondering whether they should have given more thought to a subject or an initial choice would have been better than the ultimate one. Sometimes their retrospective self-inquiry involves questioning why they stressed over something insignificant. A task-driven business executive claimed she always scrutinizes decisions she has made—from the length of the family vacation to business decisions—even though she also recognizes that her choices have been sound. The function of regret after a task has been competed is discussed in more detail in Chapter 5.

General self-observation that may take the form of regret provides an opportunity to learn, change, improve, or compensate for actions the next time around. For most things, there is a next time. Even so, people who are successful in their endeavors or careers question doing well enough or being good enough, whatever that may be. Those with high standards and a tendency to be perfectionistic are inclined to experience self-conscious emotions—shame, guilt, or pride—in their strivings.[5] Given that the pursuit of excellence is a quality among successful people, whether or not they procrastinate, Chapter 6 is devoted to this subject.

DELIBERATING ABOUT UNCOMPLETED TASKS

The more people identify with being a procrastinator, the less they are bothered by something left unfinished until a deadline is in sight. However, an uncompleted task is troublesome for a task-driven person.[6] Holding something in mind and repeatedly thinking about the task until it has been completed can be uncomfortable for them.

Researchers have attempted to demonstrate that people who put off task completion are just ignoring what needs to be done, and more recently, researchers have speculated that delay has to do with not being conscientious.[7] This may be true in the case of people who fail to complete tasks for any variety of complex psychological reasons. However, professionally successful procrastinators *do* think about tasks that must be completed, as illustrated by Sam in the beginning of this chapter. The procrastinator's ability to relax or get involved in distracting activities prior to a deadline is an important and indeed fascinating aspect of their deadline-driven style, which I discuss later in this chapter. Procrastinators organize data, particularly for written work, as they engage in what others might mistakenly refer to as "unproductive" activities. In the back of their minds, they are considering the uncompleted task while they surf the Web, play a round of golf, clean a closet, or engage in any number of unrelated undertakings. The burst of energy required to finish something appears as the deadline approaches.

What's impressive about deadline-driven procrastinators is their accuracy, so it isn't unusual to hear a story from a procrastinator that he or she incessantly delays and then e-mails an important and perfectly executed document one minute before the deadline. The secret to pulling off excellent work at a deadline has to do with procrastinators' capacity to hold subject matter in mind and deliberate. They can delay and remember well, in contrast to their task-driven counterparts, who do not want to be burdened with having to remember or fear they'll forget if they don't do it now. Task-driven people often rationalize their need for immediate action by speculating that some unforeseen eventuality may interfere with getting the task done.

People vary in their capacity to hold something in mind, although many other factors may influence a person's comfort level about needing to remember something. Cognitive scientists refer to *working memory* as the system by which the brain temporarily holds and processes information. Researchers studying this process have speculated that some people are willing to expend extra effort when they have a strong desire to get things off their minds. This was illustrated by participants in a study of working memory who exerted themselves by carrying a heavier load for a greater length of time (in this case a bucket filled with pennies) just to complete a task as soon as they could to get it off their to-do list.[8] Procrastinators might have a hard time grasping why someone would actually choose to put out extra effort just to get something done and dismissed from their minds.

Holding information in their minds until a deadline is close seems to bother procrastinators less. Delaying action should not be perceived as their lack of concern, but instead as their capacity to hold and reflect on information. When they are not tangibly working on a task prior to the deadline, they are often thinking about it and passively planning their approach prior to taking action. A news columnist explained that he absolutely cannot complete a story until the exact words of the ending appear in his mind, which is always at the deadline. He mentally constructs the story as time passes, recognizing that others may perceive him as doing nothing. Similarly, an entrepreneur explained his style of getting things done, claiming, "I look like I'm lazy and unmotivated, but I'm always thinking about it in the back of my mind." Likewise, a successful deadline-driven research analyst reported that when he tries to complete tasks ahead of time, he "can't get anything done." However, he noted he is always "actively thinking about it."

Diverting attention away from a task while holding information in working memory has been explored in terms of the process of *incuba-*

tion in problem solving.[9] Deadline-driven people describe such a process as the period in which others may perceive them as being distracted and doing nothing. However, diverting attention away from the task at hand, according to the theory of incubation, allows them to passively work on it until they are motivated by a deadline to actively engage in the project. An internal solving process that is gradual, continuous, and unconscious occurs during this incubation period, and during this time, what's going on around them influences the solution process.[10] Too much focus can harm performance. Problem solving requires both analytic and nonanalytic processes: sometimes focus is needed, and sometimes less focus is better—particularly on creative problem-solving tasks.[11]

Thus, while procrastinators are contemplating their projects, task-driven people are seeking relief from having the task on their minds. Task-driven people consider themselves to be highly organized and efficient, and as such, they generally express the importance of getting things done as soon as possible. Only when a task is put behind them can they move on to potentially enjoyable other things, that is, unless another task appears.

DISTRACTION

Distraction is common to each motivational style and includes what some people consider to be productive distractions, such as cleaning and organizing. As demonstrated above, task-driven people become distracted by important as well as insignificant uncompleted duties or chores, but they sure seem to be getting a lot of things done. Until a deadline is near, procrastinators are distracted by activities unrelated to the task to be completed, including productive distractions as well as activities they regard as a waste of time. They simply pass time until a deadline is in sight. Many self-identified procrastinators find themselves engaged in a "cleaning frenzy," using the energy they feel as a deadline nears to complete other tasks. However, they also tend to reprimand themselves for being distracted away from the task at hand. This distraction serves a very important purpose that I discuss in Chapter 7.

The distraction of task-driven people is hidden behind all of the tasks that summon them. Like an alluring nuisance, tasks themselves are distracting to them. If you are a procrastinator, you may have become annoyed by the busyness of a task-driven person in your life. Worse yet, you may have pangs of guilt as you observe their "productivity" while you're sitting back doing whatever. Task-driven people won't wait, so they may even complete tasks that a partner or coworker was intending to do later. If you procrastinate, then you may anticipate their resentment or also be baffled that a task-driven person can't relax and do things later.

Simply put, task-driven people don't relax and ignore tasks that need attention. Instead, they are distracted by things they perceive need to be done, even if those tasks could be completed at another time. For these people, psychological stress results more from their urgency to do everything now, as well as from the imagined consequences of not taking care of things immediately. A successful corporate executive illustrated the distraction and stress she experienced upon entering her home and noticing all of the tasks that she was immediately compelled to attend to: breadcrumbs left on the counter, kitty litter on the floor, a plant that needed to be repotted. She wished for what seemed impossible, that she could walk into the house, sit on the couch with her partner, and simply not care about such things. Task-driven people really do feel compelled to get it all done now. They often wonder why a deadline-driven partner doesn't notice all those things, too.

While the experience of relaxation may be the absence of compelling tasks for the task-driven individual, the true experience of pleasurable relief is in getting something done so that the unfinished task does not summon them. Even so, what may generally be considered a pleasurable activity could be distracting when it remains unfinished. Unread, mindless magazines can be a distraction to those who want to put things behind them. One task-driven man described finding a solution for not having time to read the magazines to which he subscribed. He saved the magazines to read while waiting for various appointments or during his child's soccer practice, thereby making good use of the time; yet in taking them with him, he was compelled to read them as though the activity was just another task to complete.

The more people identify as a procrastinator, the more they are able to "relax" when deadlines are distant.[12] [13] [14] Procrastination is generally described as a sequence wherein the completion of a given task is deferred while the individual's attention and focus are garnered by other activities until a deadline looms. What does a procrastinator do while waiting? Distracting oneself until a deadline is close can take many forms and may involve pleasurable activities as well as less-than-pleasurable tasks, like cleaning his or her living space. The Internet provides a wealth of possibilities for the purpose of distraction. The computer-mediated environment, according to some researchers, enables procrastinators to engage in time-wasting activity, referred to as "cyberslacking."[15] However, such judgment muddies an understanding of the purpose distraction serves in deadline-driven people. Granted, not everyone who procrastinates is also professionally successful; however, those who are successful certainly balance any period of distraction with energetically engaging in task completion prior to a deadline. Nonetheless, it's likely that guilt or shame about engaging in distracting activities has more to do with the procrastinators' anticipated or previously experienced judgment from others than what they actually feel.

Most procrastination studies focus on college students, who represent a significant number of captive participants. Researchers investigating college students' work habits and distractions assessed the amount of time students studied and when their studying occurred.[16] They found that students who procrastinated did most of their studying near the deadline and studied less. Nevertheless, performance was not affected for those who delayed. Although distracted until the deadline nears, successful people who delay are deadline efficient.

In summary, successful people may or may not procrastinate, but they rarely, if ever, miss a deadline. Both deadline-driven and task-driven people are bothered by uncompleted tasks, but task-driven people are compelled to complete tasks early to free themselves from thinking about things that remain unfinished. Procrastinators who appear to be doing nothing are instead organizing data during the time in which they are not actively working on a specific task. The process of distraction is different for each motivational style. Task-driven individuals are distracted by uncompleted tasks, whereas deadline-driven people are distracted by other activities until a deadline approaches.

What is the motivation behind these divergent ways of completing tasks? Before I get down to specifics, the next chapter deals with what motivates people generally.

Chapter 3

WHAT MOTIVATES EARLY ACTION OR DELAY?

What motivates you to get something done? Simply put, both positive and negative emotions are designed to help you focus your attention on whatever activates them. When a biologically based emotion enters your consciousness, cognition is its travel companion. Often, people confuse emotion (feeling) with cognition (thinking) because these processes arise together. Our cognitive system makes specific the information provided by emotion. That is, when an emotion is activated, the meaning you automatically attribute to it—what you think along with the emotion or in response to it—will focus the vague information that is provided by what you feel. This chapter generally conveys the emotional core of motivation before I get down to specifics.

MOTIVATION BASICS

Emotions are a powerful and efficient motivational system. Biologically, emotions are immediate and reflexive. Their activation occurs in response to a specific stimulus—a situation, an event, an image, or a thought—of which you may or may not be aware. Your brain has the ability to evaluate circumstances in the environment. If it comes across something it wants to amplify, it can, through emotion, effectively draw your conscious attention to that stimulus by making it important positively, negatively, or neutrally. When your brain activates an emotion, the various components of your nervous system create physiological and sensory changes in your body and coordinate emotional expression. The thoughts accompanying an emotion are images created by your cognitive system, as well as subsystems of perception, motor control, memory, and language that make more specific what the emotion conveys. Thus, in a general way, emotions help you to recognize or adapt to opportunities or problems and what's going on around you.

Any emotion, positive or negative, can motivate you to complete a task. You may be motivated to do something because it activates the pleasurable feelings that accompany positive emotions. On the other hand, you may be motivated to do something to avoid the feelings that may result from negative emotions or to relieve yourself from feeling their effects. This is one of the ways in which human beings are wonderfully designed: we are motivated to maximize our positive emotions and minimize negative ones.[1] Now, this does not mean we are a bunch of hedonistic pleasure seekers. Although we are built to desire good feelings, we are also equipped with emotions that can impede or disrupt our positive feeling states. You may have noticed that emotions such as shame, guilt, or disgust do a very fine job of interfering in situations when you might be feeling really good, such as when you've eaten a delicious meal but have eaten too much. We may not like feeling some of our negative emotions, but they serve an important purpose. Our avoidance of negative emotions or our wish for relief from how they make us feel not only motivates us but also keeps us in check both personally and socially. If nothing ever got in the way of our pleasure seeking, we would not have a civilization that functions very well, and we may not be mindful of imposing limits on ourselves. It's not the fault of evolution that some people do things that do not maintain the social order. Perhaps we can view such behavior as an evolutionary function gone awry.

Theorists vary, but not considerably, in their classification lists of what constitutes primary or core emotions. Most emotions have a range of intensity, which makes the experience of them quite different. For example, anger and rage are considered the same process at a biological level, but in terms of intensity and presentation, they are quite distinctive. Thus, one way to classify emotions is to combine them in such a way that the range of their biological expression, from mild to intense, is taken into account. A prominent classification system, developed by the affect theorist Silvan Tomkins, ascribes two-word names to identify most of the emotions in the classification, which takes into account this range of intensity. This model posits that there are nine innate emotion mechanisms, which are referred to as affects—the biological source of emotions.[2] These nine affects are interest-excitement, enjoyment-joy, surprise-startle, fear-terror, distress-anguish, anger-rage, shame-humiliation, disgust, and dissmell (a unique name for toxic or bad smells).

Presenting you with the numerous other classification systems would unnecessarily divert your attention. However, another system is important to mention, which is based on facial expressions and was developed by psychologist Paul Ekman, a former student of Tomkins.[3] Using distinctive universal facial expressions to form his classification of primary emotions, Ekman includes anger, disgust, fear, happiness, surprise, contempt, and sadness.[4] For the purpose of understanding what motivates people to get things done, it is important here to note that Ekman does not include shame in his list because it is not regarded as having a universal facial expression, although in terms of posture (a loss of muscle tone in the neck and shoulders and downcast face) and eye contact (averting one's gaze away from others who are perceived as potentially judgmental), shame is expressed bodily. Ekman has proposed, however, that further research could provide evidence for shame as a primary emotion.[5] Although shame meets many of the criteria necessary to be considered a basic emotion, some scholars have speculated that its omission in Ekman's classification is because of the fact that people tend to avoid discussing their experiences of shame and are less likely to correctly identify shame as an emotion.[6] Therefore, since we can become ashamed of being ashamed—even though shame is not something to feel shame about—individuals tend to hide what they feel, including from researchers.

You may wonder why many other emotions, including some of your most favorite and least favorite, are not included in these classification lists. Many emotions are subsumed under the primary emotions or are the product of two or more primary emotions that are blended together. When two emotions are activated in close proximity or one emotion is activated in response to another, you may experience any number of emotions, such as anxiety, jealousy, envy, guilt, embarrassment, love, amusement, compassion, relief, or awe, just to name a few. This blending, and the various emotions that result from it, is much like the way in which we combine two or more primary colors to produce a unique hue. Our repertoire of emotions, like all the colors in the spectrum, has its basis in the commingling of primary sources.

THE ACTIVATION OF EMOTION

An emotion will be activated when it is triggered by a stimulus—an event, a situation, a thing, or the action of another person. It's common vernacular these days to claim something has "triggered" you, implying something has happened that has messed you up emotionally because it has activated an emotion based on an unpleasant emotional memory. This notion is not far afield from what actually happens, but at a more basic level what activates an emotion can be any stimulus. The emotion directs your attention to the stimulus that activated it, whether or not you like it. One typical stimulus that would activate an emotion, for example, is the siren of an approaching emergency vehicle. As the sound becomes closer and louder, your heart begins to beat faster, and you may have an urge to look outside to see what's going on. You cared (paid attention) because you felt something. Feelings make you care. Be it mild fear, distress, or interest, the stimulus motivated you to take an action. Perhaps what you felt led you to protect or reassure yourself, or maybe you were led to satisfy your curiosity. Similarly, a task to complete is also a stimulus, whether it's a presentation to prepare for or an overflowing toilet to unclog. Some stimuli, like an overflowing toilet, generally create a sense of urgency for most of us, whereas other stimuli can more easily be disregarded.

The emotional importance we give to a stimulus influences how we will attend to it, so it's likely most people would not ignore the stimulus of their toilets overflowing because it may activate distress, startle, or disgust. If you are task driven, you may experience an emotional urgency about many things you have to do, even if they do not have to be completed any time soon. However, procrastinators will likely not experience that same degree of urgency to complete tasks until their emotions are activated by the stimulus of an impending deadline. Such variations in how people automatically respond to a stimulus might at first seem rather simple and easily altered. However, these variations in task-completion style are based on a complex network of emotional, cognitive, and physiological memories that are integrated and stored in our brains. As a result, they bias our attention and script our present behavior.

BIASED ATTENTION AND THE FORMATION OF SCRIPTS

What attracts our attention—our preferential perception—is based on the relative emotional importance of a stimulus. Theorists refer to this process as affect-biased attention.[7] The potential for emotions to bias attention has been studied in phobias, for example, where people who are fearful in certain situations are more inclined to direct their attention to stimuli in the environment that mimic those fears.[8] Thus, if you are afraid of encountering a coyote during your hike on a trail, you may be more likely to mistake another hiker's dog in the foliage for a coyote than someone who has not developed such a fear. Our attention is biased in numerous ways as a result of our experiences of emotions that were activated, or not activated, by a particular stimulus. Whereas one person, for example, may have an emotional response that always makes him or her pay attention to dirty dishes in the sink and feel compelled to do something about them, another person may not notice. Consequently, such differences are often a source of interpersonal conflict. We may not take into consideration the fact that people differ on the basis of their preferential perceptions and may instead misunderstand or ridicule their behaviors or habits.

Emotional memories help us manage our lives because they are part of the learning process. All of our experiences when emotions were triggered and how we responded to them are compiled in our brains and contribute to forming the set of rules by which we live.[9] Sequence patterns of stimuli, the emotions activated by them, and corresponding responses become *scripts*, which are much like a reflex that is coded into implicit memory and thus operate automatically and mechanically.[10] Scripts are based on the repetitive activation of a given emotion or emotions consistently activated by a particular stimulus. Thus, the compelling nature of the scripts that are formed in our minds, along with their complex psychological organization, can lead us to distort a new experience—a stimulus—to make it fit an already existing script. As such, the emotions we experience in the present have past histories that have been compressed into mini-theories that help us make sense of regularity and change in our lives and provide information concerning ways of living in the world.[11] Depending on how well we learn, scripted responses can either help or hinder us as we interpret, evaluate, and make predictions in our experiences.

Most people are well aware of some of their scripted emotional responses to situations, especially in terms of the mini-theories they have developed around intimate relationships. If their new partner behaves in a particular way, they find themselves cognitively weaving theories, based on their past emotional responses in similar situations, that inform them via their present emotional response. Often, in interpersonal situations this involves protecting oneself from the shame of hurt or loss. Since our scripts are based on what we have learned from all of our past experiences when similar emotions were triggered, we cannot necessarily undo or erase them along with our emotional memories, but we can learn further from them and modify our responses.

Scripts also begin to form early in life in relation to what motivates task completion. Your experiences around how you get things done become an integral part of the automatic and complex psychological organization in your brain that determines how you approach task completion. This is the implicit set of rules by which you live and the way in which you manage your life in terms of task completion. Likely, their origins date back to your first experiences of completing tasks, such as assigned homework: Did you feel better if your homework was completed before you played or did other things, or could you easily let your homework wait until later, or even much later, like just before class? Taking a look at the outcome of your present approach to completing tasks—whether you are a rock star or a self-declared failure—should give you an accurate indication of whether you need to make adjustments.

Scripts are rooted in our emotions, which are always filtered through our past experiences and our culture.[12] Thus, the culture and environment in which you were raised contribute to how you respond emotionally. If you live in an environment where you frequently hear the alerting noise of emergency vehicles, for example, you may respond differently to the sound of a siren than someone in an area who rarely hears one. Culture and environment as well contribute to the promotion or acceptability of particular emotional expression, so if the existence of certain feelings were denied, the ability to perceive a particular emotion may be overshadowed.[13] For example, expression of negative emotion, such as anger, is often discouraged in families, but sometimes so is positive emotion, such as excitement.

THINKING AND FEELING

When an emotion makes a stimulus important by magnifying it, that importance is transformed and held in place by cognitions—the thoughts you assign to it. So if fear is activated when you hear the siren of an approaching emergency vehicle, it will garner your attention. Concurrently, you will likely have an image or thought about where it is headed and what has happened. Your emotions placed the stimulus of a siren prominently in the arena of your attention by magnifying it and providing you with general information and motivation to do something. At the same time, your cognitive system makes the general information specific, in this case, speculating where the vehicle is going and why.

In consciousness, feeling and thinking always arise together,[14] so when you hear the siren of an approaching emergency vehicle or become aware of a task to complete, for example, your thoughts and feelings will emerge simultaneously. Cognitions that arise along with an emotion are necessary to make that information more specific. Of course, in many cases, an emotion will amplify how you feel about something, but what you think alongside of it is usually complete conjecture on your part. In a sense, what you think about something you may fear doesn't tell you what you are actually afraid of but instead provides the best information your mind has available to it. For example, you may be fearful whenever you drive across a bridge. Your cognitive response may lead you to believe that driving over a bridge is dangerous, when in fact, you are unaware of what you actually fear. However, if you believe you fear the bridge, then your fear may be triggered on subsequent trips.

In the past, many researchers in the field of psychology considered cognition to be more important than emotion in influencing attention and motivation. You will find as you read along that I emphasize the importance of emotion in how we think, which is becoming a more dominant view of what motivates human behavior. In his elaborate review of research concerning the hemispheric functions of the brain, Iain McGilchrist refers to the "primacy of affect," offering evidence that affective (emotional) judgment motivates cognitive process.[15] In our disposition toward the world, according to McGilchrist, the contribution of the left hemisphere, which involves our cognitive assessment, is influenced by our affective judgment and sense of the whole, much of the time without our being aware of that fact.

Cognitions and emotions can interact in ways that perpetuate a process. In other words, what you feel can lead to thoughts, and then what you think can trigger further emotions. This occurs when thoughts are produced initially by an emotional response, and then the thoughts themselves activate additional emotions. The interaction of emotion and cognition is important in the process of what motivates you to complete a task. Cognition alone does not motivate action unless it activates an emotion. A procrastinator may sit on the couch playing video games while reminding himself that he really should finish a report, but he has the thought without any inclination to take action, perhaps even if the thought activates only mild distress. However, upon looking at the clock and recognizing he has barely enough time to finish the task, his bodily sensations of distress linked with fear will move him. Could he have talked himself into an energizing emotional response? Possibly, but it is unlikely. Emotions can be impervious to cognition. In fact, they may be quite independent, which is why many attempts to achieve substantial attitude change through communication, instruction, or persuasion are not successful.[16] In this regard, instructing people who procrastinate on how and why they should complete tasks earlier will be ineffective. In short, emotion influences whether you are driven by deadlines or by uncompleted tasks, but to effect real change, both cognition and emotion must be considered.

EVALUATING SITUATIONS AND TAKING ACTION

Your brain's ability to evaluate situations, events, or stimuli is referred to as an *appraisal* or an *appraisal tendency*.[17] Such appraisals happen automatically, without your conscious control, and trigger a reflexive emotional response.[18] Your appraisal system takes into account your well-being, plans, and goals when it processes events or situations and provides them with meaning. Your brain scans this incoming sensory information to detect patterns associated with past situations, even before you recognize what may be happening. Thus, memory is an important contributor to our emotional responses to situations, and as such, we appraise events, both consciously and unconsciously, based on how closely the circumstance resembles past situations and patterns. As a result, certain situations will always evoke past memories, and these appraisal tendencies are the characteristic way in which your brain has learned to evaluate them. In other words, emotional responses involve both your biology and the biographical memories that amplify what you feel. For instance, if you had an intensely shaming experience in fifth grade when you raised your hand to make a comment, this experience will forever remain in your emotional memory and may color your feelings every time you command center stage to provide an opinion. Even so, present experiences that differ from those in memory, such as having subsequent positive moments in the spotlight, can dampen the future impact of unpleasant emotional experiences.

Many adult procrastinators, as children, seldom did their homework in advance and recall completing projects near the deadline, even though sometimes this last-minute pattern for completing their homework was accompanied by the distress or anxiety of a task-driven parent or project partner. When asked why they waited until the last minute to do their homework, many procrastinators say they wanted to play or do other enjoyable things. Conversely, their task-driven counterparts frequently say they were compelled to do their homework immediately after school and that only by getting their homework done first were they able to enjoy playing or doing other things. Like personality traits, scripts, or appraisal tendencies, these early life experiences of emotional states around task completion, at some point, solidify into patterned emotional responses to tasks and lead to a particular style of task completion.

MOTIVATION PROVIDED BY POSITIVE EMOTION

In the next few chapters you will discover the tremendous motivation that results from various negative emotions. There is, however, a positive emotion I would like to emphasize in this book, namely, interest-excitement. Interest, and its more intensely felt presentation in excitement, is activated when your brain evaluates a situation or event with pleasantness, desire, or a perceived need to expend effort.[19] Curiosity, exploration, and information seeking are associated with the emotion of interest, which has high value in terms of learning, which takes place throughout the human life cycle.[20] In fact, researchers found that people who use strategies to make an activity more interesting (i.e., self-stimulation) tend to view the activity more positively.[21] Although interest and enjoyment are helpful innate tools we use for task completion, the motivation we derive from avoiding negative emotions or seeking relief from them is an engine that can really drive us. This is explored in the chapters that follow.

To summarize, our motivation to do something, whether immediately or at a deadline, is based on what will maximize our positive emotions or diminish or relieve our negative emotions. Positive emotions supply us with energy and drive. Experiencing a positive emotion about anything will direct our attention toward it, whether it's something that has to be done or an activity that distracts us from a task. When a project or a deadline for a project activates a negative emotion and amplifies the urgency to complete it, we may be motivated to get it done so that we'll be relieved. Similarly, the way in which we respond when an emotion is activated also determines why we may get things done ahead of time or wait until a deadline. Finally, any emotional response in the present is influenced by our history, culture, and implicit memories of prior experiences when that emotion was activated. Now that we've covered some basics of emotion as a motivating force, let's take a look in the next chapter at the powerful role of anxiety in motivating task completion.

Chapter 4

ANXIETY AS AN ENGINE OF TASK COMPLETION

In the context of getting things done, anxiety is your friend. The aim of anxiety is to help you pay attention and provide you with energy. You may dislike the way it makes you feel, but that's the point: the primary way in which anxiety motivates you to take action involves your desire to rid yourself of its effects. When you are anxious about getting something done, for example, notice that once you have completed the task your anxiety disappears, at least until your attention is drawn to the next thing you have to do (if you are task driven) or until a deadline is lurking for something else to complete (if you are deadline driven). Perhaps beyond being a friend, anxiety is like a niggling parent who continually reminds you about something and knows you'll both be relieved when you deal with the situation.

There are undoubtedly times when normal anxiety has led you to feel a bit unhinged. At excessive levels anxiety places you on high alert regarding a perceived current or future threat. As a result, you may attribute feeling its effects to having some kind of psychological condition—becoming anxious that your anxiety means something is really wrong with you. The psychological and physiological effects of anxiety can be so unpleasant that we may disregard its important evolutionary function to protect us. Thus, there are many healthy and unhealthy ways in which people attempt to relieve normal anxiety, such as through exercise, deep breathing, avoiding sources that trigger it, the use of reassuring self-talk, withdrawing, or medicating it with legal or illegal substances.

Although anxiety may seem prominent in terms of something people experience, it is not considered to be one of the primary emotions; rather, anxiety is a blend of two or more primary emotions that are activated together or results when one or more emotions are triggered in response to another.[1] When blended with various other positive or negative emotions, the composite creates the different ways in which anxiety is felt. The dominant emotion in anxiety is fear, which may account for why many people confuse the two concepts. I briefly describe the differences in this chapter. Since any primary emotion when blended with fear can create some form of anxiety, it is no wonder that the word "anxiety" has so many connotations, including nervousness, apprehension, energy, stress, agitation, excitement, tension, and worry.[2]

My goal is to help you appreciate anxiety as a powerful engine that drives you.[3] Understanding what anxiety is all about can give you an advantage and help you succeed in what you do. This chapter gives you an overview of the emotion and illustrates the focus and energy anxiety provides through the distinctive ways procrastinators and nonprocrastinators make use of it.

THE CONFUSING CONCEPT OF ANXIETY

What actually is anxiety? From a biological perspective, anxiety is an emotional state that involves prolonged muscular tenseness and anticipatory thoughts (cognitions) that serve to regulate attention, memory, and reasoning.[4] These physiological changes and anticipatory thoughts prepare you to take action. Although the emotional message conveyed by anxiety is vague, the cognitions that arise with it attempt to clue you in to what it is trying to tell you; however, in the case of anxiety, imagination can go wild.

The concept of anxiety has a very long history, which has resulted in myriads of definitions and numerous applications. Likely, the term has been perpetuated because of Sigmund Freud's early conceptualizations of anxiety as an important dynamic in human behavior, which were published in his writings from 1895 until 1933. The anxiety Freud observed in his patients was very intense, as opposed to the generalized way we use the term presently, and might be referred to these days as panic or terror.[5]

Early on, Freud distinguished what he called *realistic anxiety*, when an actual source is present, from what he termed *neurotic anxiety*, when the source is unknown.[6] Such a distinction may seem quite plausible, given that abbreviated version of Freud's definition. However, in the context of the Victorian era, in which his theories evolved, Freud considered both types of anxiety as a toxic result of unreleased sexual desires. Realistic anxiety, he believed, is rational and creates increased sensory attention and motor tension, such as the experience of unfulfilling sexual practices or having to suppress sexual urges. In contrast, Freud maintained that neurotic anxiety was the result of sexual inhibitions, such as unacceptable desires that must be kept out of conscious awareness, that created a general apprehensiveness ready to attach itself to an idea that will justify it. So in this regard, if a person experienced anxiety about something or someone, Freud might speculate that the object of the anxiety was simply a target that served to keep hidden the actual source of the person's fear. Later in his life, Freud revised and expanded his view of neurotic anxiety, speculating that it was an intrapsychic "signal" that a present event could repeat an earlier traumatic situation.[7] Such earlier traumas, according to his theory, might involve an anticipated loss of one's mother, loss of love, castration, or a fear of punishment.

Although theories of psychological conflict have evolved significantly since Freud's time, he certainly was correct in speculating that emotional memories can be reactivated and applied to something that has triggered a similar emotion in a present circumstance. When a situation or event in your environment has the potential to activate an emotion, instantaneously your brain will scan memories of all your prior experiences of when that emotion was activated, along with your response pattern. These emotional memories and patterns of responding to a particular emotion can serve to inhibit the emotion from being triggered or amplify it.[8] For this reason, your emotional response to any scenario may differ from another person's response. Similarly, emotional memories and patterns of responding to anxiety are very present in terms of the motivation to complete tasks, whether you are inclined to take action immediately or defer action. When it comes to emotional responses, people differ in significant ways. We can always find someone who agrees with us or responds our way to an emotion, but we have to consider that many will respond differently.

Distinguishing Anxiety from Fear

Commonly, the references people make to anxiety are indistinguishable from how we describe the emotion of fear. The distinction between fear and anxiety can be confusing since in certain anxiety disorders, particularly phobias, as described in the *Diagnostic and Statistical Manual of Mental Disorders* (2013), the focus is specific and avoidance behaviors are present.[9] Although phobias are considered to be an anxiety disorder, we think of a phobia in terms of something that is feared, be it insects, enclosed spaces, heights, or contamination. Additionally, fear of the unknown, fear of death, fear of contamination, fear of flying, fear of catastrophe, fear of failure, and fear of success are all commonly noted fears, they are actually experienced as anxiety.

While fear and anxiety are related, they also differ in significant ways. As a primary emotion, fear is activated in response to an imminent threat from a known source, which immediately leads to an urge to defend yourself.[10] You would likely experience fear, for example, if while driving you suddenly saw another car careening out of control toward you. In contrast to fear, anxiety is a response to an unknown threat or to something that is not specifically threatening.[11] Distinguished from the imminent quality of fear, anxiety is a longer-lasting state of nervousness and apprehension that puts you on alert to a future threat or to the possibility of danger, such as being vigilant while driving because you anticipate there are going to be careless drivers on the road. Some researchers, for example, distinguish between fear and anxiety by determining whether avoidance behaviors are present.[12] Others make the distinction based on whether the intended outcome has to do with avoidance or escape.[13]

More important, whereas fear is a primary emotion, anxiety represents a blend of emotions in which fear is dominant.[14] The commingling of other emotions, along with fear, makes anxiety a response to a vague, nonspecific threat, as opposed to a fear response when the source is known and avoidance of danger is required immediately.[15] The blending of fear with other emotions to produce the variety of ways in which anxiety is felt and how these variations of anxiety are often used to get things done is discussed next.

THE BLENDED NATURE OF ANXIETY

How anxiety feels depends on what other emotions have been activated along with fear and, thus, commingle with it. Along with fear, the other emotions your brain may activate to produce anxiety may include, for example, distress, shame, anger, disgust, and excitement. Because your emotions have been modified by your experiences and culture, you will have a unique quality of anxiety.[16] Let's take a look at some of the various flavors of anxiety and how you might experience them in the process of completing a task.

To start, and relevant to this book, if you have anxiety about having many things to get done or little time to do them, the anxiety you feel likely involves a coalescence of fear and distress. Generally, distress itself is felt as agitation, annoyance, or tension—a constant and unpleasant sensation that may arise from a variety of internal and external sources. When you are distressed, you are motivated to anticipate what's going to go wrong and then try to solve the problem effectually.[17]

In fact, when it comes to getting something done, distress can be useful. For example, manufacturers may create mild distress to evoke an emotional response in the consumer so that the consumer will pay attention and respond accordingly. Consider the simple example of getting into your car, starting the engine, and hearing the constant chiming that alerts you to fasten your seat belt. Ultimately, the annoyance of the dinging sound will motivate you to seek relief by fastening the belt. Tasks to be completed can produce the same effect if distress alone is activated; however, even greater motivation will result if your brain combines the distress with fear, shame, anger, or disgust, for example. Yet unlike the signal to fasten your seat belt, the "dinging sound" of distress anxiety is internal and can be deflected until it is activated by a deadline in people who procrastinate or serve to incite immediate action in those who are task driven.

When you have limited time or much to do, you might describe anxiety as a feeling of stress or tension. Feeling stressed or "stressed out" is the result of distress that has been activated in response to fear, which is very prominent in the mix.[18] The concept of stress itself encompasses both positive and negative conditions that can affect one's psychological and physical well-being. Current research suggests that how a person responds to stress determines whether the stress is harmful.[19] Your body is preparing you for action, so the tension you feel serves you best if it is directed toward action that will alleviate the stress. Otherwise, if you feel distress and become further distressed because of how you are feeling, the emotion becomes amplified.

A second "flavor" of anxiety is worry. Worry is the cognitive side of distress, and it magnifies the distress component of anxiety. Professionally successful people, regardless of their task-completion style, worry similarly about uncompleted tasks; however, the action they are compelled to take as a result of their worry differs considerably.[20] Worry creates immediate stress for task-driven people, who tend to be more continuously stressed than their deadline-driven counterparts. After all, procrastinators are able to relax and for a time, put aside a task. Nonetheless, worry does reside in the back of their minds until they are motivated by a deadline. Even so, to their task-driven counterparts, they may seem unperturbed until the deadline is on the horizon.

Fear and distress also activate and commingle with the emotion of excitement. When this occurs, you may feel aroused, stimulated, or in the zone. For task-driven people, the stimulus that causes such arousal may be the need to complete multiple tasks, or it may accompany intense focus. For procrastinators, time pressure can create such arousal. In a study of adept students who procrastinate and subsequently cram for exams, the cycle of calculated procrastination, anxiety, climactic cramming, and victory was characterized as a peak performance of personal best and as an addictive high.[21] I'll say more about arousal a bit later in the chapter.

An emotion that you would not ordinarily consider as a motivating force in task completion is disgust. When disgust is activated along with, or in response to, fear and distress, the melding produces disgust anxiety. Disgust by itself is highly motivating. At a basic level, disgust is a rejection response to something that tastes bad or just doesn't sit well. Disgust causes you to experience something as revolting or repulsive—making you want to expel or avoid it. This emotional response is designed to protect you by motivating you to get rid of, or distance yourself from, whatever is offensive.

When your brain adds disgust to fear and distress, you become anxious about encountering something disgusting, or you may experience it as a fear of *being* disgusting—namely, that someone will perceive you or something associated with you as disgusting. Thus, in an effort to minimize the possibility of repelling another person, you will be motivated to do something about it. I mentioned previously that it is erroneous to conclude that self-identified procrastinators always do such things as leave household chores, such as dirty dishes, until much later. All emotions motivate us, and there are factors other than a deadline or being immediately attentive to tasks that might compel someone to wash dishes, including disgust anxiety. As one procrastinator explained, "When I look at a sink of dirty dishes, I feel disgusted and so I wash them." Procrastinators who have task-driven partners will likely tell you their partners don't give them an opportunity to deal with dirty dishes because, of course, their partner has to wash them right away. Chapter 7 may help you find ways to address this issue.

If you are grumpy and agitated in the process of getting something done, your unique blend of anxiety may include anger along with fear and distress. Both deadline-driven procrastinators and task-driven people commonly experience agitation—they become such a grouch—in the process of getting things done. Since anxiety results in highly focused attention on a task, interrupting them may trigger an eruption. Procrastinators have limited time and their focus is intense, so when a partner makes suggestions or recommendations that are contrary to how a task is being completed at the deadline, or if a partner requests that something in addition be completed within the deadline, they may be subjected to a negative outburst from their partner. It often occurs that when task-driven people are partnered with people who are deadline driven, the task-driven partners tend to believe they are the only ones who get things done. Their anxiety about tasks to complete becomes flavored with agitation that is triggered by thinking the burden of certain mundane tasks—be it cleaning, bill paying, or scheduling—is all on them.

The blending of various emotions that produces anxiety also makes it possible to experience the emotion as both positive and negative at the same time. You may have experienced that effect on an amusement park ride, while engaged in a challenging sport, or when you anticipated seeing someone who is a romantic interest.

RESPONDING TO ANXIETY

Generally speaking, when a particular stimulus—a situation or event—triggers an emotion, on a biological level it is a momentary episode, so you may wonder why some emotions, like anxiety, can hang on so long. This happens in part because whenever an emotion is activated, emotional memories and cognitions arise that are based on prior experiences. The impact of these prior experiences may serve to either extend or magnify the duration of the emotion.[22] Therefore, an infant will not experience anxiety in situations that might activate anxiety in an adult, such as hearing an approaching siren, yet as children grow up, they learn from experiencing an emotional response to a stimulus or situation. Thereafter, their brains activate a specific emotional response that is associated with a stimulus, event, or situation. Such links reside in an array of emotional memories stored in the brain. At the same time that the emotion is activated, we also will automatically express or inhibit an emotion based on our emotional memories and what we've learned from our culture or environment about what is acceptable or appropriate for expressing the emotion. As well, based on our particular environment or culture, we learn as young children what's beneficial, permissible, or unacceptable in the way an emotion is expressed. These memories and learned responses to emotional expression are why one person may not exhibit anxiety about something, whereas another person will become highly anxious.

As an example, imagine you randomly choose one hundred people and have each of them be a passenger on a somewhat challenging taxicab ride. Likely, you will find a variety of responses to how anxiety is experienced and expressed. Some people will clearly be anxious, and the anxiety will show in their behavior, such as tightly holding the handle of the passenger door. Others may have had experiences that inhibit the activation of anxiety, and thus, they may pass the time attending to the route or other things. Yet upon reaching their destination safely, these people, who did not outwardly exhibit concern, may nonetheless enjoy relief at the moment when they step out of the cab. Passengers who live in major cities and are familiar with challenging cab rides may remain relatively calm. Doubtless, several of them may respond to what they feel by yelling at the driver to slow down or to be more cautious, whereas others will issue a more passive and polite request. A few may find their anxiety intolerable and insist on stopping prior to arriving at the destination, and then there may be at least one passenger who loses his or her lunch all over the back seat.

Similarly, there are variations in the ways in which people respond to anxiety when they become aware of a task that needs to be completed. Patterns of experiences and memories in the emotional life of task-driven people will compel them to act immediately when anxiety focuses their attention on uncompleted tasks. On the other hand, when they know that a task can be delayed, deadline-driven procrastinators will not experience the same anxiety; rather, they will hold these pending tasks at bay, along with a muted anxiety in the back of their minds until a deadline intensifies their anxiety and motivates action. As mentioned previously, emotional memories of situations in early formal education, such as a pattern of when a person completed his or her homework, can solidify a temporal style of task completion.

Contrary to task-driven people, anxiety is a highly intense, but time-limited, experience for procrastinators. Conversely, task-driven people maintain a continuous level of anxiety because the emotion draws their attention to uncompleted tasks until each task has been completed. An approaching deadline significantly raises the intensity of their anxiety; however, they generally do not have the benefit of the skills developed by procrastinators in navigating deadline stress and task completion. Thus, from their perspective, procrastination behavior may appear to be unhealthy because of the stress it creates as the deadline approaches. However, we must ask, is it actually more stressful to experience a time-limited intense burst of anxiety or a continuous level of anxiety? In truth, probably neither is better nor worse than the other. People simply have differences in their experiences and expressions of emotions that motivate them.

How fortunate, for procrastinators at least, that until a deadline is near, they are able to defer the anxiety of uncompleted tasks that is activated in task-driven people. Some people who are deadline driven are able to relax before a deadline is near, seemingly devoid of tension. Others shift the focus of their anxiety to something other than the task at hand. In either case, an imminent deadline to complete a task is necessary to trigger sufficient, and often intense, anxiety that will provide the drive to get it done.

ANXIETY AND THINKING

Anxiety, in fact, can motivate you in positive ways. For example, anxiety can facilitate learning and intellectual performance.[23] However, the adaptive and motivational value of anxiety has often been obscured by negative perceptions of the emotion, which has led to some misconceptions regarding when the tensions associated with anxiety should be blocked and when they should be encouraged.[24]

One of the great assets of anxiety is that it compels us to focus our attention on the stimulus, as noted in the discussion of attentional bias in Chapter 3. So if you are in a state of high anxiety, your attention becomes directed toward whatever you think is its source. As such, the emotion you experience actually amplifies the source and takes your attention away from other things.[25] Therefore, in a situation of time pressure, the narrowed thought process results in a better focus on a specific problem and leads you to be less susceptible to distraction.

Cognitive scientists who have studied anxiety and the motivational basis of working memory—the system of memory that holds information in your mind while you manipulate and process it—have found that anticipatory anxiety can actually motivate thinking as opposed to being a distraction, as many may assume.[26] Thus, if you are task driven, the recognition that a task has not been completed may activate anxiety that will garner your attention. If you procrastinate, anxiety will focus your attention as the deadline nears. Consequently, you will disregard all other distractions that previously had occupied you. This enhanced narrowing-of-attention scope then leads you to preferentially zoom in on smaller regions of space.[27] Many people describe this process as "being in the zone."

To date, anxiety has been studied primarily in terms of how it impairs thinking rather than how it acts as an adaptive mechanism that can narrow and focus attention. For example, many procrastination researchers have found high levels of anxiety in people who delay task completion until deadlines are upon them, which researchers have associated with maladaptive or undesirable behavior.[28] Thus, these studies have tended to characterize anxiety as an aversive motivational state, and as such, these researchers would recommend that a person would do well to reduce the effects of anxiety to achieve a goal rather than use this emotion as a source of energy and motivation. As an example, researchers found that a significant number of students who procrastinated in preparing for examinations reported considerable anxiety.[29] Yet rather than explore this anxiety as a motivating force in task completion, instead they suggested that people should attempt to reduce their level as a procrastination intervention. These researchers completely missed the point that the effective and adaptive use of deadline anxiety would be completely negated by such an intervention!

Based on these procrastination studies, common recommendations for performance anxiety have involved calming techniques to decrease arousal. More recently—and more in line with the observation that anxiety can enhance performance—reappraisal techniques have been found more effective than anxiety suppression.[30] These techniques help people to reevaluate and reframe their experience of anxiety, from being distressing to being exciting. Since both ways of experiencing anxiety are anticipatory and characterized by high arousal, your ability to reappraise a state of negative arousal as being positive is, in fact, easier and thus more effective than attempting to shift from an anxious state to one that is calm.[31] Such cognitive reappraisals during stressful experiences promote adaptive responses.[32] Since cognitions and emotions arise together, interpreting what you experience as anxiety that involves the emotion of excitement, rather than just fear and distress, could make a difference in your approach to a task. This technique is discussed further in Chapter 8. In the meantime, let's take a look at the positive arousal component of anxiety and the circumstances under which it optimizes task completion.

ANXIETY AND AROUSAL

The subject of arousal and its effect on performance has been studied in relation to motivation, anxiety, and attention. You may have noticed in the examples of Judith and Ryan in Chapter 1 that each of them had a high level of arousal. Maybe you've recognized times when your own level of anxiety seemed ideal in terms of giving you energy to function effectively and efficiently—or just to get something done.

There are optimal levels of arousal in learning and performance, and tasks requiring exceptional persistence and/or endurance typically require a particularly high level of optimal arousal as a means of increasing motivation to complete the task.[33] Decades ago researchers found that learning is associated with actions that involve optimal stimulation.[34] In sport psychology, this concept became known as *zones of optimal functioning*—the notion that athletes have an optimal level of anxiety, either low, medium, or high, at which they perform at their best.[35] What's important to note is that anxiety is viewed as highly motivating and energizing, which is exactly why emotions have everything to do with task completion.

Flow, which is characterized by complete focused motivation, is among the most rewarding subjective experiences in learning and performance.[36] When we are "in the flow," our emotions are harnessed, and we are motivated to carry out a challenging behavior (e.g., athletic performance), which in turn increases our competence. Researchers have speculated that procrastination is an effort to experience flow by being under pressure to complete a task,[37] and not surprisingly, successful people do tend to experience flow in the process of task completion, regardless of their task-completion style. Illustrating this process, a deadline-driven consultant explained that limited time leads him to experience "flow, laser focus, and amazing intuition," which enables his success. He says he wishes he could feel the kind of energy he has during these periods all the time. A deadline-driven marketing executive reported that time pressure—combined with completing many less desirable tasks all at once that he had saved up—made the process stimulating for him. Similarly, a task-driven physician recounted that efficiently attending to many competing tasks that garnered her attention resulted in feeling a sense of flow.

Although both task-driven and deadline-driven people experience heightened emotional states during task completion, to date only procrastinators have been targeted in studies that seek to understand such behavior. Unfortunately, studies do not consider the potential positive effect of intense emotions as being sources of energy that motivate task completion. Instead, the research has been geared, for example, toward attempting to demonstrate that "arousal" or "thrill seeking" are simply motives for procrastinating.[38] In one comprehensive study, the researchers expected to find that procrastinators were more likely than nonprocrastinators to have arousal-based personality traits, but they failed to find significant differences.[39] Nevertheless, ignoring the role of emotions in motivating behavior, these researchers published an unfortunate and erroneous accusation that "individuals who claim that they are motivated to procrastinate because they believe they work better under pressure are likely fooling themselves, providing a seemingly believable explanation to excuse their procrastinatory behavior."[40]

In actuality, racing the clock emotionally stimulates those who procrastinate. Since emotions serve to direct one's attention, we might consider such deadline stimulation highly adaptive as well. Moreover, procrastinating enables some people to perform at peak efficiency,[41] and their task delay enables them to work diligently and attain optimal efficiency.[42] Professionally successful procrastinators report that when they try to get something done ahead of time, often they are compromised in terms of both motivation and concentration. Thus, for procrastinators, the energizing quality and focus provided by emotions that are activated upon nearing a deadline are essential.

Researchers tend to be surprised when their studies reveal that successful students procrastinate. In an investigation of academic procrastination and course anxiety, a researcher noted "an extremely disturbing finding" that a large proportion of graduate students who represented the upper echelon of academic achievers with a mean grade point average of 3.57 had reported that they *nearly always* or *always* procrastinate on studying for examinations and on weekly reading assignments.[43] Actually, this finding is not surprising at all. By effectively using time pressure as a stimulus, procrastinators activate anxiety, which motivates them to get things done.

To summarize, anxiety in all of its presentations is the engine of task completion. It provides focus, directed attention, and motivation. However, the point at which an individual's conscious and unconscious appraisal of a situation results in the activation of anxiety, which, in turn, initiates action, varies both temporally and qualitatively from one person to the next. Thus, on one hand, the recognition of an uncompleted task may, for task-driven people, trigger anxiety, which then motivates task completion independent of a deadline. In contrast, the necessity of appraising a situation as having a close deadline is what triggers the motivational anxiety for those who are driven by deadlines to complete a task.

Another version of anxiety, one that is very familiar to successful people, occurs when both shame and distress meld with fear to produce *shame anxiety*.[44] Shame anxiety is usually accompanied by thoughts of potential failure and humiliation. Thus, the cognition associated with shame anxiety is often described as a *fear of failure*. In fact, shame anxiety is highly motivating, and the following chapter is devoted to exploring it in greater depth.

Chapter 5

WHY YOU SHOULD FEAR FAILURE

Alex worried that being a procrastinator might jeopardize his career as a trial attorney. Even so, he is always completely prepared and performs exceedingly well in court. As deadlines approach, however, Alex's anxiety becomes magnified and his fear of failure becomes increasingly acute. In the midst of a bout of deadline angst, Alex decided to see his physician, in addition to scheduling an appointment with a psychoanalyst the same week. Explaining his anxiety as a result of his tendency to procrastinate and his fear of failure, the physician suggested a psychostimulant medication to help Alex focus on his work. However, Alex objected to taking medication as a solution. Next, he consulted with the psychoanalyst, who speculated that Alex's procrastination and fear of failure were likely a result of "unconscious hostility" toward his father. Alex subsequently declined the psychoanalyst's recommendation that he attend multiple weekly treatment sessions. Thus, Alex decided he would live with his "symptoms," and as always, he just got the work done.

Regrettably, health care professionals have perpetuated the erroneous belief that a fear of failure, especially when it accompanies procrastination, is maladaptive, symptomatic, and an indication for pharmaceutical or clinical intervention. While in the throes of deadline anxiety and fearing failure, many procrastinators like Alex do worry that something must be wrong with them. Perhaps for this reason, coupled with their own biases, psychological researchers have attempted to explain procrastination as a pathological behavior that is *due* to a fear of failure.

Some researchers, for example, speculated that a fear of failure is the result of evaluation anxiety, low self-confidence, and overly perfectionistic performance standards, which then lead people to procrastinate.[1] Yet many studies investigating the possibility that a fear of failure leads people to procrastinate have had mixed results.[2] For example, in a survey of university students regarding their reasons for procrastinating, the fear of failure was not implicated by procrastinators.[3] In fact, successful task-driven people also have a fear of failure and often appear equally symptomatic when they are anxiously doing everything they think has to be done immediately. Indeed, a fear of failure is significantly present among those who are successful in their careers, regardless of whether they self-identify as a procrastinator.[4]

SHAME ANXIETY

The emotions that accompany the images of failure are a huge source of motivation for many successful people. There are a number of specific emotions that coincide with the thought that you are going to fail. The prominent emotions are anxiety (distress combined with fear, as explained in Chapter 4) and shame. In fact, shame is the core emotion of fear of failure.[5] When shame commingles with distress and fear to produce *shame anxiety*, the resulting emotional mix can be a powerful motivating force.

Shame anxiety is experienced as a fear that exposure is imminent and humiliation will soon follow.[6] Experiencing this intense emotion signals that action must be taken at once to diminish its intensity. Thus, if you are compelled, or eventually compelled, to do something or get something done to get rid of the effects of shame anxiety, then the combination of emotions has served its evolutionary purpose. Unfortunately, in a study where the fear of failure was found to motivate individuals to succeed, the researchers nevertheless regarded the fear of failure as a maladaptive characteristic along with "laziness" and "postponement of work" in those who procrastinate.[7]

In everyday activities, a fear of failure is motivating. Anticipating a negative evaluation or judgment from yourself or others—like the thought of being embarrassed, which is a derivative of shame—can focus your attention on accurately and efficiently completing whatever it is you need to get done. If there is an optimal level of shame anxiety that helps people to complete tasks, it would be up to each individual to determine that level for himself or herself. This is because any emotion a person might feel at a given moment has been modified by the individual's culture, experiences, and responses to situations where that same emotion was activated. As a result, there are people for whom a fear of failure greatly contributes to behaviors that ensure their success, and there are others whose response to the commingling of distress, fear, and shame leads them to fail.

When task-driven Mark is negotiating a potentially lucrative deal, for example, he becomes nervous and worried about the humiliation he would feel should he fail, and this incites what he refers to as "strategic thinking and intense attention." Similarly, Annette, an account executive who procrastinates, experiences anxiety whenever she secures a major account, becoming preoccupied with the thought that it will be her last. This preoccupation leads to images of financial ruin and personal disgrace that then transform into a need for immediate action to pursue other accounts. In other words, Annette's images of failure, the cognitive side of her shame anxiety, create an assumed deadline and motivate her to act immediately to relieve her negative feelings. In contrast, Carlos struggles with a fear of failure in his belief that he must live up to the image of his high-achieving father. Rather than motivate him to get things done to avoid the possibility of failure, his response to shame anxiety, instead, is a defensive one. The anxiety that he will be exposed to the shame of failure leads Carlos to avoidance behaviors where he drinks excessively. As a result, he fails to complete important tasks and responds to the shame he encounters by blaming others, including his parents, whom he perceives as expecting him to achieve high success. When shame is prominent in one's life, anything that can reduce the image of others or another's self-esteem assists the individual to feel better about himself or herself.[8] Moreover, any shame resulting from the reticence that prevents a person from action is reduced by the use of alcohol or drugs, which temporarily dissolve shame.[9]

Shame permeates our existence and affects our personal identity in profound ways. Having a better understanding and awareness of this emotion will give you a basis to recognize what's behind the fear of failure. Besides, even a cursory understanding of shame can give you a tremendous advantage in your personal and professional life. The significance of shame in interpersonal relationships, specifically regarding divergent motivational styles, is addressed further in Chapter 6. For now, let's get a better understanding of shame, responses to the emotion, and how shame anxiety can motivate you.

THE NATURE OF SHAME

Shame is more expansive than you can imagine, and it permeates professional, educational, and interpersonal situations. Further, what activates feelings of shame may not always be experienced as you would expect. The most familiar understanding of shame is that it is the emotion activated by any threat to your esteem—your established sense of self. In such circumstances, shame is felt as exposure to the judgment of another person or yourself—a sense of shrinking or being small or a feeling of being flawed, inadequate, unworthy, or out of control.[10] So when shame is activated, it is accompanied by thoughts of being an incompetent person. Generally speaking, these thoughts are about one's personal identity with respect to physical and mental adequacy.[11] Therefore, shame is the emotion you are experiencing when you imagine not being smart enough, attractive enough, strong enough, or skilled enough. Further, emotional transformations of shame, such as when it commingles with distress and anger to produce envy or jealousy, may be activated to signal that your self-esteem is threatened and motivate you to protect yourself or achieve goals that are represented by your perceptions of other people—to have what they have or to be like them in order to feel adequate.

Shame is also activated when positive emotions, such as interest, excitement, enjoyment, or joy, are partially impeded or obstructed, when we are expecting the positive feelings to continue.[12] You probably never thought about shame in this particular way, so let's reflect on a couple of examples. First, let's consider an example of shame as an impediment to positive feelings as it pertains to procrastination and the fear of failing. Suppose Bill, a procrastinator, has an important project to complete. He is excited about the possibility of going on a river-rafting trip with his brothers and is completely caught up in researching various locations for the expedition. Suddenly, he feels a pang of shame. Simultaneously, he is seized by the thought of an approaching deadline for an unfinished project. Becoming aware of his concern that he will fail unless he starts on it right away, he is motivated to get to work.

Consider the purpose of a negative emotion interfering with the continuation of a positive feeling. Here, we can see how Bill's shame interrupted his pleasurable activity and shame anxiety helped motivate him to complete a task. Thus, as unusual as it may seem, shame has, in fact, an important evolutionary and adaptive purpose: essentially to interfere with positive emotion and make us pay attention to the source of the shame. If we take this a step further, suppose that nothing ever interrupted your enjoyment or interest. You might not be aware of threats to your survival—like having a good time and not being vigilant about the possibility of a saber-toothed tiger salivating near your cave. Shame, in this sense, gives us a very stringent message to bring us back to reality.

Often, shame is triggered in a situation when you are experiencing positive emotions in an interaction with another person. As a result, your enjoyment immediately diminishes. Imagine Dustin and Marissa, who recently began dating, are at an outdoor café, having coffee and an enjoyable conversation. Marissa suddenly feels herself recoil and notices that Dustin is not quite listening to what she is saying, distracted by an attractive person sitting nearby. The internal wince she is feeling in this situation is the activation of shame. It is the result of her brain's recognizing the disconnection, even before she was consciously aware of what was going on, and by triggering shame, it instantly reduces the intensity of the positive feelings she had been experiencing. Hence, the information shame has given to her will motivate her to pay attention and protect herself. There are many possibilities in terms of her response. Later in this chapter I discuss the various responses people have to shame and shame anxiety.

The good news is that shame only *partially* impedes positive feeling. At the same time, shame also motivates us to restore the positive feelings we derive from interpersonal connection, so in the case of this example, Marissa may be motivated to do something that will reengage Dustin, make an excuse for his behavior, or ask whether something is wrong between them. Alternately, the shame she feels from the interaction may lead her to have an angry response. Even though anger seems to create a distance between people, it often results in a preoccupation with the relationship that negatively maintains the bond. Emotions make us care, and we care whenever we feel.

The activation of shame based on the disruption of a positive interpersonal connection is experienced early in life, and how we learn to respond to it affects later relationships. Loss of connection or feedback from caregivers, and the child's response to it, is what we experience as shame later in our lives. Very young children, in the midst of an exciting moment, may notice that their parent has become distracted or disengaged. Shame, then, develops in response to our caregivers' facial expressions, such as in the absence of their smile when they fail to convey positive emotion to us as we had hoped or expected they would—as well as in their vocal tones when the quality of their voice suggests disengagement or rejection.[13]

Visualize a two-year-old child who is expecting that a particular behavior on his or her part, like dancing wildly or acting silly, will elicit a joyful response from a parent as it has in the past. Instead, this time, the child's parent happens to be distracted—by a phone call perhaps—and possibly is unresponsive or annoyed as well. Thus, shame is activated in the child, resulting in disappointment, frustration, anger, or withdrawal, among other possibilities, in not having been acknowledged by, or attuned with, the parent as the child had been in previous situations that were very gratifying.[14] In our adult life, such painful emotional memories influence our current state when we worry that we have failed to achieve a goal or when a desired bond with another has been broken.[15] Thus, the experience of shame is based on caring about what others may think. Since we are subject to experiences of shame because we care, the emotion also motivates us to restore the bonds that feel broken.

At this point, and especially if you are a parent, you may wonder whether any unintentional behavior on your part is damaging if it subjects your child to shame. That's just not the case. Shame experiences are inevitable, but more important, early shame experiences, and how we learn from them, provide us with information in terms of how to respond when shame is activated in adult life. Ideally, we learn from shame experiences if we can talk about what we feel and reestablish any lost connection to a loved one rather than respond to shame in maladaptive ways.

Generally speaking, we have little conscious control over these often very intense sensations of shame, which has led some theorists to consider shame akin to an acute stress response.[16] On a physiological level, we experience shame—and show our shame—in our face in an unusual way: we attempt to remove our face from the interaction.[17] We'll turn our face away and avert our eyes, and our head and neck lose tonus, causing us to slump.

The anticipation of a painful emotional state—as well as images of loss of self-value that accompany the physiological sensations involved in shame—makes shame anxiety a powerful motivational tool for humans. In essence, people are highly motivated throughout their lives to "save face." If people anticipate that they will feel shame in a particular situation, they will be on high alert. Thus, in considering the many sources of shame and its significant role in motivating our behavior, notwithstanding a fear of failing at task completion, our early memories of shame experiences become reminders of why shame is something to avoid. So it is reasonable that we might become anxious about the possibility of experiencing shame, even to the point of developing some level of shame sensitivity. Researchers have even found that sensitivity to rejection that results from experiences of shame may develop earlier than cognitive sources of rejection, such as the social comparisons we form in childhood.[18]

SHAME COMMINGLED WITH OTHER EMOTIONS

Emotions that are activated along with or in response to shame can transform how shame is expressed. Fear and shame together can create the facial expression of guilt as well as terror, excitement combined with shame can produce a seductive look, distress and shame appear as both sadness and failure, and anger combined with shame creates an expression of unwilling defeat.[19]

Shame is often confused with guilt. However, unlike shame, guilt is an emotion brought about by something you've done about which you might feel remorseful and wish to make amends. The violation of ideals is associated with shame, in contrast to guilt, which is generally considered to be associated with the violation of a social standard.[20] Put another way, shame is about the quality of who we are as opposed to guilt, which is about actions or laws and is felt whenever we act in a way that harms another person or violates a social code.[21] Some emotion theorists consider shame and guilt to be self-conscious emotions. With these emotions, the evaluation of your behavior, according to some standard, rule, or goal, may lead you to the conclusion that you have failed—in contrast to a third self-conscious emotion, pride, which leads you to conclude that you have succeeded.[22] The unique characteristic of self-conscious emotions is their role in self-regulation. In this regard, shame, guilt, and pride provide internal feedback about meeting or violating your expectations, goals, or standards.

One way to understand guilt is to recognize it as an emotion that arises from the simultaneous activation of shame and fear or the triggering of fear in response to shame. Guilt does encompass the shame of actions that have caused harm to another person or violated some rule or law, but it also contains some degree of fear that our behavior will result in retaliation on the part of the person who has been wronged by our action.[23] At other times, distress is activated in response to shame. In this case, the shame of one's actions that have hurt another person is accompanied by empathy for the person who has been harmed, which then activates distress in the perpetrator.

The experience of regret results from the blending of shame with fear and distress. In the case of regret, shame is triggered by an awareness of one's action, which is accompanied by a fear of punishment for the behavior and distress that are produced by the constancy of shame.[24] Consider a time when you might have experienced intense regret based on some action you took (including inaction). A quality of regret is that the emotions producing it are repeatedly activated, making it difficult to rid yourself of the thoughts associated with regret—you may obsess about your wrongdoing and its potential consequences. Thus, regret is felt as a preoccupation with the shame of what you have done wrong, along with the fear of what may happen as a result, to the point of causing you distress.

Despite how negative regret may feel, it represents internal feedback about performance and serves an important self-supervisorial function. Although taking a look at one's performance may not necessarily influence future behavior, retrospective assessment certainly has the potential to provide a learning experience. According to cognitive scientists, the orbitofrontal cortex—a region in the frontal lobes in the brain—plays a fundamental role in mediating experiences of regret.[25] The cognitive process, known as *counterfactual thinking*, has to do with our assessment of what was gained compared to what would have been gained had we made a different decision.[26] Thus, the regret experienced by successful task-driven and deadline-driven individuals alike may represent an important dimension of their capacity to review their performance retrospectively and thereby learn from it.

In Chapter 2, we see that successful people, regardless of their motivational style, have moments of regret following the completion of tasks, often looking back and speculating how they could have performed better. However, some researchers take for granted that procrastinators would (or should) experience more regret than nonprocrastinators. An example of one such study examined regret experienced by procrastinators in various life domains.[27] This study found procrastinators to report significantly more regret than nonprocrastinators in the domains of parenting, family and friend interactions, health and wellness, financial planning, and education pursuits but not in career-planning, romance, spiritual, and self-improvement domains. Even so, successful people tend to learn from regret based on their experiences of shame. In spite of, or perhaps because of, how terrible shame may feel, it is a "teacher" that enables us to look within ourselves and leads us to think deeply about ourselves.[28]

RESPONSES TO SHAME ANXIETY

There are various ways in which people respond to shame anxiety vis-à-vis completing tasks. Some may quit or withdraw effort, whereas others—including our successful task-driven and deadline-driven individuals—push themselves to succeed in an effort to avoid the shame of failure. Examining fear of failure in the context of research pertaining to an academic setting, researchers found that a fear of failure drives many students to achieve and persist in the face of challenge and adversity.[29] These researchers view the motivation provided by fearing failure as a difficult and uncertain emotional turmoil that includes anxiety, perceptions of low control, and unstable self-esteem. Even so, they also found that this kind of failure avoidance was common among university students. Some students, however, who avoided the implications of failure through lack of effort that "excused" their failure had lower achievement or withdrew from their studies.

Whether or not they procrastinate, high achievers who see themselves as effective and competent are motivated by shame anxiety. People will do many things that may appear misguided or, at the extreme, not in the best interest of their survival to avoid experiencing shame in the eyes of others.[30] This is particularly the case in the arena of education, where many students will push incredibly hard to succeed because they wish to avoid failure at all costs.[31] When students believe they are capable, coupled with their commitment to a future goal for which their grade or the course material is relevant, a shame reaction will likely result in increased motivation.[32] In short, taking action and being driven to achieve move people toward realizing their goals and evading humiliation.

Humans are motivated by their strong desire to avoid foreboding negative emotions. However, shame anxiety does not motivate everyone to achieve or complete tasks. We have seen that successful people are quite adept at using shame anxiety as a motivational tool. However, for others, shame anxiety instead results in a number of undesirable outcomes, including impediments to learning, obstructions to the motivation to achieve, and an interference with intellectual engagement. Shame anxiety may even be a contributing factor to unhealthy interpersonal relationships. Just as apprehension about the possibility of shame, for many people, is the basis behind the achievement of goals, there are some who respond to the emotion by withdrawing effort. Comments from teachers are enlightening in such situations; for example, when a teacher's evaluation of a student includes remarks such as "He's so bright . . . if only he would do the work," chances are that shame anxiety has motivated the student to withdraw rather than be motivated to expend the effort it takes to succeed. In short, not all people who delay task completion are successful. Similarly, not all people succeed because they complete tasks immediately. For those who are not as apt to succeed in either case, shame anxiety may be concealed behind actions that hide a very negative self-perception, such as failing to complete tasks adequately.

When you consider that shame is the most distressing element in the fear of failure, the motivation enlisted to hide or deflect it makes sense—shame is an emotion that everyone dreads. There are four general response patterns that people use to defend against shame when they cannot make use of the information it provides. These responses include withdrawal, avoidance, attacking the self, and attacking others.[33] They can be brief responses to a temporary moment of shame or become scripted as chronic, habitual structures within the personality. In any case, their aim is to assist individuals to restore their prior state of positive emotion. Although these defensive and coping responses to shame may not help people in the long run, at the moment shame is activated, such responses can deflect the harsh effects of the emotion and help them maintain a positive sense of well-being. Whether the defensive response involves getting intoxicated, isolating from others, being self-deprecating, or blaming someone else for what they feel, for the moment it will deflect the toxic effects of shame.

When we withdraw in response to shame, we are hiding ourselves from others and may also experience feelings of depression.[34] Even people who do succeed in their endeavors or careers are not immune from wanting to withdraw from time to time. Pulling the covers over their heads, they may dread pursuing the completion of a task or wish for a way to get out of the responsibility of getting it done. They may engage in deadline extension fantasies or escape fantasies as described in Chapter 2. Even so, successful people eventually relieve their negative feelings by attending to the task.

Avoidance is another coping response to shame, in which we want to hide our feelings from ourselves. This response may take the form of risky behaviors involving alcohol, illicit substances, food, casual sex, or any number of other ways to disavow shame.[35] Some people will respond to fear of failure or the potential of experiencing shame in other self-defeating, avoidant ways. For example, they may simply fail to meet their deadline or complete the task. In contrast, others with the same foreboding consequences looming over their heads will use them to drive their pursuit of success. Successful people may employ avoidance in response to shame anxiety, yet in time they will recognize their defensive responses and attend to the task at hand and get it done.

Even more potentially self-injurious than avoidance in response to shame are attack-self responses because this type of response involves hurting oneself either psychologically or physically. Attacking oneself may involve denigrating self-talk or, at the extreme, behaviors such as self-mutilation or suicide.[36] When it comes to task completion, having excessively high standards can result in an attack-self response, which can be manifested through extreme and unrelenting self-criticism, a sense of self-defectiveness, or feelings of inadequacy when standards are not attained. People who exhibit attack-self responses often lament they can't do the work, are going to fail, or are generally inadequate as human beings. Sometimes tears or the appearance of resignation accompany their behavior. Again, even though successful individuals may doubt themselves and exhibit such behaviors from time to time, in the end they always get their work done.

Similarly, the attack-other response to shame or shame anxiety can also be hurtful, but rather than directing the hurt toward oneself, it is expressed outwardly toward others. Encompassed within the attack-other response mode are blaming, bullying, and physically harming another, as well as general stances of aggression or attack, whether real or imagined.[37] The goal in blaming others for one's own anticipated failure is to disown the shame or shame anxiety that is felt at the time. In addition, one may make attributions about others that are disguised attempts to restore a positive self-view, such as focusing attention on the inadequacies of others and exaggerating them in an attempt to feel better about oneself. Often, the trigger that leads one to respond to shame in an attack-other mode of functioning is the sense of being powerless and alone. In these situations, people feel endangered because their self-esteem has been so significantly reduced and they risk exposing an incompetent self; thus, in a burst of rage, they believe they will prove their power, competence, and stature.[38] In everyday situations of getting things done, people who are experiencing a fear of failure may lash out at others when they are attempting to complete a difficult or challenging task.

Interestingly, much of the research investigating the various reasons people procrastinate has to do with behaviors that likely are motivated by defensive responses to shame and shame anxiety. Some of these studies involve an investigation of procrastination and a work-avoidant goal orientation,[39] distress regulation,[40] neuroticism,[41] task averseness,[42] avoidance motives,[43] fraudulent excuses,[44] self-handicapping,[45] role conflict,[46] a means of avoiding shame and guilt,[47] and a fear of failure itself.[48]

The vast majority of these studies, however, do not consider shame or shame anxiety directly. A closer look at the emotional life of those who fail, their motivational style notwithstanding, could involve many of the behaviors mentioned above that researchers have considered in their attempts to study procrastinators. Moreover, these studies were not designed to explain why some people procrastinate and successfully complete tasks, whereas others procrastinate and do not succeed. To determine why some fail in their endeavors, study participants would have to be separated on the basis of those who are successful at task completion, whether or not they procrastinated in the process, from those who do suboptimal work or fail. Regrettably, because these studies do not separate those who are successful from those who fail, an understanding of why delay does not work for some people is lost, as is an understanding of the motivational impact of emotion in getting things done.

People can become consumed by a cycle of failure and shame, wherein every failure amplifies the shame they already feel and chronic shame interferes with their efforts. As we know, procrastination is an insufficient excuse for missing a deadline and failing. Nevertheless, the many studies that link procrastination in general with all sorts of personality traits are a missed opportunity to determine what actually interferes with the motivation of those who fail and blame it on procrastinating.

Consider Lauren, for example, who described her pattern of missing deadlines, explaining that when she becomes aware of things she has to get done she just ignores them. When a deadline approaches she avoids what she feels, as well as the task, by drinking heavily and watching movies. Her attack-other response to shame results in thoughts such as *Screw it, I hate those people anyway and just won't do it.* In her last two jobs, Lauren was warned that she'd be fired for neglecting her responsibilities, but she left before it happened: "They were lousy jobs anyway," she noted. Lauren has spent years refusing help based on the fact that when she was in school her parents "forced" her to have tutors and therapists whose time she "wasted." The actual repetitive and intensely shaming experiences that led to a cycle of failure beginning early in her life were never addressed.

Some procrastination researchers might identify Lauren as a procrastinator, accusing her of possessing any of the qualities previously mentioned that have been studied in efforts to determine why some people delay. In that case, she might be regarded as a "lazy, task aver-

sive, fraudulent, self-handicapping slacker with low-conscientiousness."
Such personality assassination hardly provides insight into Lauren's defensive adaptation to deeply internalized childhood shame. However, it
does illustrate that focusing on personality traits of so-called procrastinators like Lauren obscures the emotional states that repeatedly lead
them to miss deadlines.

As a therapist I have worked with numerous but less extreme versions of people like Lauren, all of them self-identified procrastinators
who miss deadlines. As a graduate studies professor I have also men-
tored students who, unlike Lauren, have managed to achieve success in
spite of their internal shame demons and tendency to let deadlines pass.
Although many people self-identify as procrastinators because they miss
deadlines, they are not deadline driven if motivation to complete a task
is absent when a deadline is imminent. Instead, emotionally, something
has gone awry. Yet frustrated therapists, professors, or even procrastination researchers, as a result of their own shame that is activated by their
helplessness to understand these people or help them to successfully
meet deadlines, will instead attack them for being lazy or for having low
conscientiousness. Shame can be toxic. It is frequently a large but hidden component of clinical depression, anxiety, and personality disorders. When deeply imbedded shame becomes solidified into certain
personality traits and their corresponding behaviors, it challenges the
individual's potential to look with interest at what has happened and to
learn from it.

In misunderstanding—or failing to fully appreciate—the importance
of emotion, theorists have viewed shame avoidance as only a negative
trait rather than a way in which evolution has provided humans with a
useful tool to reach desired goals. Shame anxiety, as it is experienced
cognitively in a fear of failure, has tremendous potential to energize
people and help them do what has to get done. From an evolutionary
perspective, we also can appreciate this emotion as a response that
helps us learn from error or failure and can lead to positive behavior
change or corrective educational experiences.[49] Enduring the loss of
face intrinsic to states of shame and being able to recognize and learn
from the emotion, which is discussed in Chapter 8, is essential for
success.

By now I hope you recognize that a fear of failure is actually a
motivational force that can help you with task completion. Shame anxie-

ty is the emotional counterpart to the thought of fearing failure. Shame is experienced when there is a partial disruption or obstacle to our continued positive feelings and cognitively it is experienced as a sense of inadequacy, unworthiness, or as being inherently flawed. We experience shame because we care to restore the good feeling. However, rather than learn from shame, there are times when we defensively respond to it through avoidance, withdrawal, or attacking ourselves or others. Nevertheless, shame is a great teacher, and shame anxiety can be exceedingly motivating in terms of task completion.

Another focus of procrastination researchers regarding the fear of failure has to do with the notion that procrastinators fear failure because they are perfectionistic. However, perfectionism also tends to be a trait of successful people generally, regardless of their tendency to procrastinate or not. The following chapter explores the pursuit of excellence and its role in task completion.

Chapter 6

PURSUING EXCELLENCE

Successful people want to do things very well. It won't surprise you, then, that they tend to think of themselves as somewhat perfectionistic.[1] Consistently, they set high, yet attainable, standards and goals. This version of perfectionism is a quality found in both deadline-driven procrastinators and task-driven people, although the process they use to attain their goals differs considerably. What motivates people to pursue excellence in what they do? Whether we anticipate feeling the joy of pride or hope to avoid the sting of shame, our emotional system provides us with the motivation needed to get something done and do it well. Even so, both failure and a ruthless pursuit of perfection may hide an individual's extreme shame sensitivity and represent shame avoidance.

Considering perfectionism or the pursuit of excellence from the perspective of emotions is critically important to an understanding of the motivation behind it. The behaviors that people refer to as "perfectionistic" range from a healthy inclination to get things done very well to disordered behaviors that involve unrealistic standards and expectations representing unhealthy extremes in an individual's emotional functioning. The concept of pride, in contrast to shame, also provides insight into the pursuit of excellence among high-achieving individuals.

THE CHARACTERISTICS OF HIGH ACHIEVERS

High-achieving people tend to be perfectionistic in terms of their performance and goals. Optimally, their elevated ideals and expectations for success are also realistic and attainable. To that end, they may actively seek out challenging situations that provide opportunities to raise their level of performance.[2] Not all high achievers do well under stressful circumstances. Those who thrive in pressured environments have resilient qualities: they take personal responsibility for their thoughts, feelings, and behaviors and are committed to personal development and mastery.[3]

As an example, consider deadline-driven Mitchell, who is recognized by his peers as an industry leader. Mitchell underscores his desire to maintain that position. However, because he is a front-runner and the competition in his business is brutal, he explained he often feels as though he has a target on his back. Mitchell admits he has a strong desire to succeed—to have what he does be the best. When deadlines to submit contract proposals are approaching, the imagined humiliation of failing to achieve his goal, often focused on a fear that something will not be carried out to his standards, leads to him become "extremely tense and tightened up." At such times, his office becomes a chaotic scene as he and his staff scramble to ensure everything is completed to perfection. Although Mitchell recognizes that his inclination to procrastinate, coupled with an intense managerial style, is hard on his staff, he rewards them for the success of his organization, expresses heartfelt appreciation for their long-term loyalty, and gives them the credit they rightfully deserve for their efforts to close lucrative deals successfully.

Task-driven Rose also has perfectionistic standards, both as an internationally recognized professional and in her home life. Rose describes being meticulous in her work, sometimes preferring to do things herself rather than delegating to her assistants. She knows that colleagues and friends admire her achievements, but she is also doubtful that they realize the extent of her efforts and the stress that accompanies her need to do things right away and perfectly. Her favorite pastime is to host dinner parties, for which she begins her preparations a month or more in advance. She wants everything to be perfect, and making early preparations gives her time to reevaluate the menu as well as the presentation of her home. She realizes that people really do not care whether there is a unique candle in the entryway or what's served for dinner and that she bases her standards on what feels good to her.

As we have seen, deadlines represent a challenge for high-achieving procrastinators—to complete something to perfection under the constraints of limited time. Conversely, high-achieving task-driven people are motivated to get even the most insignificant things done right away, so for them, any uncompleted tasks beckon them. Challenges are erected frequently, and their version of perfectionism has more to do with how much they can do in whatever time they have to do it. Thus, task-driven people can be a bit smug about how much they are always doing in contrast to their perceptions of the procrastinators in their lives. In situations where their interest in a task is limited or not intrinsic, negative emotions serve as motivational tools, which call them to complete tasks they find to be less compelling.

The pursuit of excellence is often driven by an individual's attempt to evade anticipated shame. We are highly motivated by shame, shame anxiety, or any blending of shame with another emotion, as described in Chapter 5. An upside of shame is that it motivates a devotion to endeavors and an intense focus on goals. The experience of shame also has a very positive side in that it is a catalyst for subsequent self-evaluation, introspection, and self-improvement—qualities that are often characteristic of successful people. The activation of shame explicitly or implicitly taps into our warehouse of memories having to do with issues of competence, acceptance, ability, and worth. Thus, shame, or the anticipation of encountering how awful it feels, provides plenty of opportunity for self-assessment and learning. Even so, the negative emotion involved in the motivation to achieve may result in the use of defensive and coping responses, such as withdrawal, attack self, attack other, or avoidance, as discussed in Chapter 5.

Those who are extremely driven to succeed often are living with a core of shame handled by avoidance—shame that is masked by a veneer of sophistication and hyperintellectualism.[4] Their toxic feelings of shame are reduced when they seek to overcome any perceived personal defects through self-enhancement or success, as though present accomplishments will remove past deficits.[5] In such an effort, they might attempt to increase their self-esteem by accumulating material goods or achieving new levels of ability, competence, beauty, or wealth to disown internal shame.[6] Similarly, many people become driven to avoid shame, all the while maintaining the perception that they have overcome the limitations of childhood adversity.

Shame avoidance motivates the perfectionistic and driven behavior of professionally successful people in their pursuit of excellence, but that does not imply it is necessarily something that is negative or pathological. As noted in Chapter 5, many studies have attempted to link perfectionism to a fear of failure, but only with procrastinators, speculating that perfectionism represents *why* people procrastinate. Later on in the chapter, I present some of these studies. First, let's understand people who are highly motivated to pursue excellence. You will find that both deadline-driven procrastinators and task-driven individuals who are successful in their endeavors are prone to have characteristics of perfectionism. For the moment, it is important to suspend any value judgment you may have about being perfectionistic; instead, let's understand its emotional underpinnings.

BENEFICIAL PERFECTIONISM

The notion of beneficial perfectionism may seem oxymoronic. Granted, perfectionism has been associated with a plethora of pathological conditions, including depression, eating disorders, relationship issues, personality disorders, and sexual dysfunction. However, perfectionistic strivings can be adaptive and positive. Definitions of perfectionism and how it is measured have been widely debated in the literature.[7] In most conceptualizations, a range exists from, on one end of the spectrum, a more adaptive or healthy perfectionism, to the other, marked by extreme pathology in how people think, feel, or behave. But where does one draw the line between what is healthy and what might be considered pathological?

Researchers and clinicians recognize that perfectionistic behavior can be beneficial, and many delineate between adaptive and maladaptive types or between normal and neurotic types.[8] Adaptive or normal perfectionists have high, but realistic, performance expectations and standards. Such people are likely to pride themselves on being perfectionistic since the term, for them, represents having highly valued goals. These successful people are able to control unhealthy self-criticism, and they have the ability to feel capable and satisfied when their high standards are met.[9] Within the normal and adaptive range, perfectionistic behaviors involve striving for high standards that are achievable: devoting your time to things you care about, identifying what works and what doesn't, and considering how to make improvements.[10] Here, we can recognize that perfectionism, at optimal levels, can help both procrastinators and nonprocrastinators reach their goals and learn along the way. Aside from being perfectionistic in any realm, "perfecting" one's motivational style requires adaptation that is informed by self-supervision.

In contrast, perfectionists who are viewed as maladaptive or neurotic tend to self-critically evaluate their adequacy in meeting expectations of performance.[11] This pathological side of perfectionism involves the tendency to set and pursue unrealistically high standards and goals for oneself. Since these standards and goals can never be met, one is constantly subjected to failure and shame.[12]

Some theorists have expanded the understanding of perfectionism by using a multidimensional approach that differentiates several types of perfectionism. In one multidimensional method, for example, three types of perfectionism were identified: other-oriented, self-oriented, and socially prescribed perfectionism.[13] In other-oriented perfectionism, the individual sets unrealistic and perfectionistic standards for others and critically evaluates their performance. Self-oriented perfectionism turns the critical evaluation on the self, with the expectation that one must meet one's own unrealistic standards. The third type of perfectionism, socially prescribed perfectionism, has to do with the pressure to be perfect to meet the assumed excessively high standards of significant others. Of the three types of perfectionism, only self-oriented perfectionism has adaptive potential, often leading to resourcefulness and constructive striving.[14] This conclusion makes sense if you consider that you can neither impose your standards for yourself on others nor base your own self-esteem on your perception of societal standards or the mandates of others. Each person, then, sets standards for himself or herself, even though it is often relieving to assume those standards belong to others or to society at large. Nonetheless, shame anxiety, as experienced in the fear of failure, involves the perceptions of one's external world as a source of motivation. Given the potential to lose face if one fails, shame anxiety motivates many people to succeed.

PERFECTIONISM AND FEAR OF FAILURE

A fear of failure is thought to motivate the behavior of perfectionistic individuals in ways that maintain their high standards.[15] The multidimensional approach to perfectionism has been used to study the relationship between perfectionism and the fear of failure. Socially prescribed perfectionism is linked with beliefs about aversive interpersonal consequences of failing, such as experiencing shame because other people who are important to you may lose interest or you may upset them.[16] Researchers found that the fear of failure was more likely to motivate socially prescribed perfectionism than either of the other forms of perfectionism.[17]

As discussed in Chapter 5, shame anxiety and its associated cognition, a fear of failure, is highly motivating and adaptive. In perfectionism, however, shame anxiety can be excessive, leading to emotions that are disordered. Extreme levels of perfectionism can be a risk factor in clinical syndromes, such as eating disorders, obsessive-compulsive disorder, social phobia, or depression. In such cases, a person's perfectionistic behaviors represent an extreme level of shame anxiety, indicating a need for psychotherapy. However, at an optimal level, shame anxiety can propel an individual forward, such as in the case of Mitchell or Rose, where the perceptions of others, as well as their perception of themselves, motivate behaviors that result in successful outcomes.

PERFECTIONISM AND PROCRASTINATION STUDIES

Many studies have attempted to demonstrate that procrastination results from a tendency to be perfectionistic. In an effort to not bore you with the details of all of these studies, the bottom line is that procrastination has never been definitively linked to perfectionism. I highly question attempts to link perfectionistic traits with only those who procrastinate since professionally successful task-driven nonprocrastinators equally endorse being perfectionistic.

Nonetheless, researchers want to find the key to why people procrastinate, and they make well-meaning and intuitive assumptions in an attempt to find out what in the world would motivate someone to behave in this way. I believe they actually wanted to discover why some people fail to meet deadlines, and they assume it is because perfectionistic tendencies, along with a fear of negative evaluation from others, leads some people to let deadlines pass them by. Once again, I want to caution you not to associate failure with procrastination. Certainly, it is plausible that people who have perfectionistic standards may fail because they cannot imagine doing what it takes to reach their goals. In any case, procrastinators do not own perfectionism. Task-driven people can be just as perfectionistic as their deadline-driven counterparts. They may even believe that their constant attention to what has to get done or how much they get done in a given amount of time is a perfectionistic quality that is superior to the behavior of their deadline-driven peers, who seem to be relaxing or attending to other things. The fact is that procrastinators are often getting things done in their heads. Unlike task-driven people, they don't take up a lot of time reversing their decisions or going back to correct errors when they finally do perform.

Nevertheless, some of the authors who have studied procrastination and perfectionism have made very important, although passing, observations about their results. In one study, the authors noted the possibility that, for some people, procrastination may be a stronger indicator of psychological health than psychological distress.[18] Well, finally! In a similar study where the authors did not observe a reliable direct relationship between perfectionism and procrastination, the authors suggested that greater attention should be devoted toward the role of emotions in discerning the causes, dynamics, and consequences of frequent task-completion delays.[19] At last! Although their quest was for indicators of pathology, they were on the right course in suggesting that future research should consider the role of emotion.

More recently, procrastination researchers have attempted to link procrastination with low levels of conscientiousness as measured by the scale of the five-factor theory of personality.[20] Personality facets that are measured by the scale include competence, order, dutifulness, achievement striving, self-discipline, and deliberation.[21] Conscientiousness is highly correlated with self-oriented perfectionists—those who set high standards for themselves rather than believe they must meet a high standard that is determined by others.[22] Since conscientiousness is often linked with perfectionism, an assumption that is out there in the world of psychological research is that low conscientiousness and perfectionism result in a tendency to procrastinate, or to put it another way, that procrastinators have low levels of conscientiousness and are perfectionistic in a self-defeating way.[23] Granted, this may be true for people who fail to meet deadlines (those who are referred to as procrastinators). More important, though, it may represent a false accusation made about procrastinators, since in their process of delay they may not appear competent, orderly, dutiful, or self-disciplined! Successful people who are early in the procrastination cycle would undoubtedly score poorly on the five-factor theory of personality scale. The content of the conscientiousness scale consists of nine items for which the extremity of each item is rated on a five-point scale ranging from "Disagree strongly" to "Agree strongly." The items, prompted by the statement "I see myself as someone who . . . ," include stems such as "Is easily distracted" (reverse scored, but a no-brainer for procrastinators who see themselves as distracted until a deadline is in sight), "Tends to be disorganized" (this item is reverse scored for conscientiousness, but based on societal standards of how "well-organized" is defined, procrastinators would definitely assume they diverge from the norm), and "Tends to be lazy" (reverse-scored item that procrastinators would endorse based on their guilt or shame about waiting for deadlines).[24]

I know I've said this before; however, it is worth repeating. In any studies that have to do with people who procrastinate, including the more recent studies regarding the trait of conscientiousness, it is critical that procrastinators be differentiated from those who fail. Those who fail may indeed have traits of low conscientiousness that cause their delay; their tendency to procrastinate is not what bites them. Likely their low conscientiousness has to do with emotional issues that lead them to not care about what they do or do not get done. Nevertheless, assigning personality traits, such as low conscientiousness, to people who fail is a value judgment that does not help them. Low conscientiousness means you don't care. As I have stated before, emotions make us care and we care because we feel. Failing because one "does not care" represents a complex emotional issue that can be overcome with well-deserved psychotherapeutic intervention. However, if you ask people who are successful and procrastinate whether they care about the outcome of their work, without a doubt they will answer affirmatively. Once again, unfortunately, people who fail and blame it on procrastinating (although we know other things are going on with them) are not separated in studies from those who procrastinate and succeed. Just because someone procrastinates does not negate that he or she has high standards. Successful people who procrastinate do have high standards, and these standards may be a reflection of their high ideals generally, much like their task-driven counterparts. A person who represents well the sentiments of successful deadline-driven individuals made the following succinct comment: "People who know me know I'm really conscientious. In fact, I am very conscientious. They just have to wait, and they know I always do on time what has to get done."

PERFECTIONISM AND MOTIVATIONAL STYLES

Overall, healthy perfectionistic traits are found among successful people, and perfectionistic strivings are not necessarily regarded as indicators of poor psychological adjustment. However, when perfectionists believe that their acceptance from others is contingent on being perfect, they often do not experience pride when they succeed, and they also experience more shame and guilt following failure than nonperfectionists do.[25] Both task-driven and deadline-driven people tend to identify with having traits of perfectionism; however, they respond differently to their perfectionism. Those who are task driven tend to become overly concerned about doing something exactly right and, as a result, have a tendency to change their minds several times before they are satisfied with an outcome. They would have a difficult time completing tasks at a deadline because there is not enough time to recheck their work or answers or alter their decisions. Things need to be finished, put away, or cleaned up. If they do review their work, as most successful task-driven nonprocrastinators tend to do, they will find something to improve on. Eventually, they decide it's enough.

In contrast, deadline-driven people tend to wait until they are aware of exactly what they want to say or do, and they have a strong tendency to complete tasks "perfectly" the first time—at the deadline. They may delay while thinking about how they might perform or complete a task, but when they actually do so, they do so with confidence and firm conviction. They do not necessarily need time to review their work since the execution is itself an end point of the deliberation that goes on in their heads beforehand, as described in Chapter 2.

At optimal levels, shame anxiety as it manifests in perfectionism contributes to successful task completion. In a study of evaluative threat—in this case, being evaluated in a writing task—researchers examined the role of perfectionism in the participants' cognitive, emotional, and behavioral responses.[26] Compared to nonperfectionists, perfectionists assigned the task greater importance at the outset and reported higher levels of negative emotions regarding the evaluative component, yet they were more likely to report that they should have done better. These results are similar to the characteristics noted by successful task-driven and deadline-driven people who often experience regret following task completion, which was discussed in Chapter 5. People who can learn from their mistakes, or what they perceive as a situation where they could have performed better, are often those who are most successful in their efforts. Unfortunately, in some cases, people have not developed the skills required to learn from shame. We can refer to this self-reflective capacity as resilience, or an ability to respond nondefensively to error. Unhealthy perfectionism can lead people to assume they know already what they have yet to learn, set goals that are unachievable, hide inadequacies from themselves and others, and become trapped in their perception of what is perfect.

In summary, successful people tend to be perfectionistic, whether or not they procrastinate. Although we often consider perfectionism to be associated with pathological conditions, perfectionistic strivings can be regarded as positive and adaptive. Perfectionism is associated with shame anxiety and the avoidance of shame. Only procrastinators have been studied in terms of perfectionism, yet successful task-driven people, as well, tend to be perfectionistic.

Now, let's turn to interpersonal situations where deadline-driven procrastinators and task-driven nonprocrastinators have difficulty navigatating through their differences and understanding each other. You can learn a lot about yourself and your relationships with others if you are able to reflect on situations where different motivational styles create conflict. The next chapter focuses on the impact of divergent motivational styles in intimate partnerships, in the workplace, and between parents and their children.

Chapter 7

RELATIONSHIPS AND DIVERGENT MOTIVATIONAL STYLES

Intimate and work relationships can be challenging when the people involved have different styles of getting things done. If you've been in one or more of those relationships and are aware of the challenges, you may be tempted to defend the merits of your own motivational style as you read this chapter. So before you get to that point, for the time being put yourself into the psyche of people who do things differently. You do not have to accept their way of doing things, but only consider their perspective.

Undoubtedly, the behavior of people with a motivational style that differs from your own can be annoying or even trigger your anger. There may have been times when you avoided interacting with them or withdrew and did not communicate much while collaborating on a project. Just as a task or a deadline can activate emotions, the behavior of other people, especially those who complete tasks differently than you do, may also be a stimulus that triggers uncomfortable emotions in you. As with all emotions, you are provided with information and motivation to take action. However, in interpersonal situations where emotions speak to you, their vague message can be misinterpreted and responded to in ways that disrupt a bond you have with another person. Navigating through differences in task completion, or anything else, may seem rather difficult at times. Nevertheless, in the process of doing so it's possible to learn a lot about yourself and better understand someone else who approaches things differently.

NAVIGATING THROUGH DIFFERENCES

What can you do when an unpleasant emotional response is triggered in an interaction with someone who has a style that is different than your own? You can understand your emotional response and effectively communicate with the other person. Later in this chapter I give you some basics for doing so.

Generally, procrastinators and nonprocrastinators often clash based on *when* something gets done. Usually, such conflict occurs because each person in a relationship has his or her own sense of timing in terms of when something should get done, and each assigns value to it. There is no superior way of getting something done if you evaluate task-completion situations using the criteria that deadlines are met and the completed work reflects the person's best efforts. High-quality work that is on time is a consistent goal. With this in mind, it is irrelevant whether something is completed on the early side or at the deadline.

Nevertheless, task-driven people often don't trust a deadline-driven partner or coworker to complete something or do a good job when the deadline is upon them. They also assume procrastinators reap the benefits of task-driven promptness without having to help reduce the workload. In intimate relationships, task-driven people may also assign a particular value to the timing of a procrastinating partner, so they may assume their partner does not care about them enough to get something done right away. A task-driven person, who of course, prefers to make plans in advance, may take personally what he or she perceives as a lack of planning or a failure to make plans as far in advance as is preferable for him or her by someone who is deadline driven. However, in such cases, a deadline-driven person will have his or her own negative response to each other's differences. Procrastinators have a difficult time understanding the urgency of task-driven people. It appears to them that this urgency is impulsive, interferes with setting priorities, and compromises outcome. They may assume a task-driven partner is trying to make them feel guilty about not immediately participating in a task or is always too busy to interact.

Task-driven parents rarely trust a deadline-driven child to get something done on time. As a result, a task-driven parent may become angry and nag or worry that his or her child will not be successful if the child does not get things done right away. Meanwhile, the deadline-driven child may experience shame or anger in response to shame about a parent's lack of faith in his or her way of doing things or react negatively to a sense of being overly controlled. As a deadline approaches, the child's expression of anxiety—the same anxiety that motivates him or her to complete a task successfully—may be met with further anger by the task-driven parent or a lecture that includes "This wouldn't be happening if you had started earlier." As well, procrastinating parents may not understand what compels a task-driven child to complete tasks ahead of schedule. They may instead view a child's task-driven nature as overly anxious or compulsive behavior, especially if the child's desire to get something done seems to interfere with the parents' agenda or goal.

Emotions can aid communication in these circumstances, but unfortunately, based on imagination that accompanies feelings, one can run amok with the attributions made to another person's behavior. In any situation that involves a relationship with another person, making assumptions about his or her behavior—and believing the conclusions you derive from those assumptions—usually leads to conflict because you'll be wrong. Instead, let's be interested and curious about what's going on with a partner or child who approaches the completion of tasks in ways that seem very alien to your own style. In the same way, when you intensely experience an emotion, be interested in and curious about what you are feeling before you jump to conclusions based on what you automatically and cognitively assign to it.

In interpersonal situations, intense emotions and corresponding thoughts may lead each party to make inaccurate assumptions and accusations regarding the other person's behavior. As we take a look at situations where task-completion differences between people end up in tension or conflict, you might find it useful to know the general communication guidelines I have applied to them. There are many approaches to effective communication. The following guiding principles of communication, adapted from the work of psychologist J. Samuel Bois, are helpful to consider in any interpersonal conflict:[1]

1. Whether you like it or not, accept the other person for who he or she is at the moment—his or her values, purposes, opinions, feelings, and goals, which may or may not change in the course of the encounter.

2. Expect and invite the other person to reveal himself or herself, to freely express feelings, purposes, values, fears, doubts, information, or interpretations related to the situation.
3. Express your own reactions similarly, making clear that all you express is subject to correction and elaboration in the light of the exchange with the other person.
4. Maintain and enhance a friendly feeling mood that will keep you and the other person in felt contact with each other.
5. Do not critically evaluate the other person's views against your own as the standard of truth and wisdom, but take his or her views as a tentative standard against which you reexamine and reevaluate your own feelings and opinions.
6. Put aside any purpose you may have to discover some elusive objective solution to the problem. Rather, see the process as a mutual attempt to reach a higher level of wisdom, separately and together.
7. Measure the success of the communication experience, not by a victory for the individual views you held prior to the encounter, but rather in terms of the increase in mutual trust and achievement of a willingness to help each other that were discovered while navigating through the difficult and/or touchy situation.

WORKPLACE DIFFERENCES IN TASK COMPLETION

The immediacy experienced by task-driven people who just want to get something crossed off their lists and dismissed from their minds can be very disruptive and agitating to deadline-driven procrastinators, who hold tasks in their memory, trusting they'll get to them in due time. As a result, they usually do not understand or value the early-bird behavior of task-driven people. Inaccurate assumptions about efficacy are sometimes made based on who gets there first. This is the case in many different contexts, and certainly so in the world of business and management.[2]

Where procrastinators tend to produce a finished product at a deadline, task-driven people are likely to create a draft of their work, modify it themselves, or assume a coworker on the project will make modifications later. If completing a task is their primary goal, task-driven people may believe it is done, when, in fact, it can be improved by further work. Revisiting or reviewing what they have written will often lead task-driven people to submit revised documents. These revisions will likely annoy deadline-driven coworkers because those who procrastinate tend to complete work in one draft. Thus, if you receive an e-mail with the subject line "Read this one instead," the sender is likely task driven. Conversely, if you receive an e-mail with an attached document very close to the deadline, it's probably from a procrastinator.

Kevin, who is deadline driven, has learned to adapt to one of his task-driven business partners. As he explained it,

> He's the first one out of the box when the firm has a project, always in a hurry to get his part done. There's an anxiety level he has where he just seems to have to complete things and get them behind him. I really respect his contributions and appreciate how he thinks, but what he produces could be better organized. I've just gotten used to rewriting his part. I used to become very annoyed with him and it got in the way of our work. We talked and came to an understanding that it's just what's going to happen. He will give me what he's got and I'll get the document in perfect shape . . . at the last minute, of course.

In contrast to Kevin's adaptation to his task-driven business partner, consider Judith, the advertising executive we met in Chapter 1. Judith would complete a task, cross the item off her to-do list, rewrite her list on a clean sheet of paper, and with pleasure and relief, toss the old version of her to-do list with the distracting scratched-off item into the trash. Early in her career, Judith realized that she encountered conflicts with her associates when the resolution of a pending task required action by someone else. At times such situations were agitating, interfered with her concentration on other tasks, and even interrupted her sleep. In paying attention to the reactions of her business associates, she recognized she was imposing on others her value of completing something immediately. Now, she restrains herself from her tendency to inquire repeatedly about the status of a project by reminding herself that positive relationships with others are more important than clearing her to-do list.

In the workplace, people may tend either to be acquiescent about motivational style differences or to become frustrated about the way someone else gets things done. Task-driven people who believe they get more done than peers who procrastinate may consider it unfair if their peers are equally valued in the organization and, worse yet, that they get away with doing everything just before a deadline. Procrastinators may not appear to be working on a project or an issue prior to an approaching deadline, and sometimes they are not. However, we generally interpret the behavior of others according to our own standards, values, and way of doing things. If you are task driven, the incubation period for the procrastinator is time wasted. If you are a procrastinator, the constant urgency of a task-driven person is time wasted as well. Instead, when you apply the neutral standard that deadlines are never missed and work quality reflects one's best efforts, the perspective changes.

More beneficial still would be to gain an acceptance of differences, discuss them with coworkers, and together learn how to navigate them. Paul, who is a managing partner of a large organization, explained how he and his coworkers have acclimated and learned to accommodate their divergent styles. He noted, "It has taken a long time for some of the people who work with me to realize that I always do what has to be done and never miss a deadline but that I may not do it right away. Now, they don't ask me for documents in advance unless they're absolutely needed. But when they do ask for something, I know they need it right away, and I make certain they have it. Instead of anyone getting upset, it's now an understanding, and even sort of a joke, among us."

How would you evaluate the performance of coworkers who *do* miss deadlines? Whether you procrastinate or not, if you are successful at meeting deadlines, it's likely you would evaluate their performance as inadequate. Participants in a study evaluated the performance of a nonexistent contrived colleague who was late for business deadlines that would affect the company's productivity.[3] The researcher was surprised to find that people who identified as procrastinators were more inclined than nonprocrastinators to blame the contrived colleague and not external factors for poor performance. Unfortunately, the researcher did not consider the fact that successful people who procrastinate are effective at meeting deadlines, and therefore, *of course* they would be critical of someone who misses them. Instead, the researcher speculated that blaming the colleague was reflective of the procrastinators' projection of displeasure regarding their own inadequacies and thus they believed that the target (even though similar to themselves) should be punished.[4] This particular study of procrastination in the workplace, specifically the researcher's speculations, illustrates the confusion that occurs in studies when procrastinators who are successful at meeting deadlines are not separated from those who miss deadlines.

PARTNERSHIPS AND CONFLICTING STYLES

If you have a different motivational style than your partner, you may find it hard to tolerate some of the things your partner does or doesn't do and his or her timing in general. Sharing a home with another person may be difficult for a variety of reasons, but would you be surprised to learn that having different task-completion styles ranks high on the list of agitating things that create conflict? Nathan, for example, uses the spare bedroom as a work area. When his wife, Katie, negatively comments about it, he feels misunderstood, becomes frustrated, and points out to her all the things he has to get done that are organized (in her opinion, they are scattered) on the desk, bed, and around the room. Occasionally, at such times, Nathan will counter with a remark about one of Katie's annoying habits. Nathan became concerned when Katie flew into a rage and threatened divorce so that she "could live alone and not have to look at this crap all over the place." She was tired of worrying that their home would be a mess when people came over. However, Nathan maintained that her concern and edginess were completely unfounded. He wished Katie could understand how much he has on his plate and that it's just the way he works. Besides, when people are going to visit he always puts everything away.

It's easy to understand why task-driven people would assume that their deadline-driven partners would forget to do something. Because their own attention is drawn to uncompleted tasks, rather than rely on remembering, they just get things done. Therefore, they may issue reminders to a partner who procrastinates or simply complete the task themselves. In any case, a partner who procrastinates may perceive such behavior as insulting, intrusive, or guilt provoking. Consider Miguel, who is offended by his partner's constant reminders to him about pending tasks. He always knows exactly what's on his mental list and precisely how long the tasks are going to take. What annoys him most is, when a deadline nears and he starts on his part of the project at hand, that's the moment his task-driven partner reminds him about what he has to do. What's more, she then tells him about other things that need to be done as he is trying to focus on the first task. Miguel often feels that life with his task-driven partner can best be characterized as a gigantic to-do list that has to be tackled immediately.

Household chores are often a sore point when it comes to divergent styles of task completion. Ellen and Dina, who have difficulty negotiating household tasks, provided a good example of this issue. Ellen said she had reached her limit of doing most of the housework while chores seemed to go unnoticed by Dina. In frustration one evening, rather than do the dishes immediately after dinner as was her preference, Ellen announced to Dina that she was leaving the dishes for her to do. She then patiently waited until bedtime, all the while restraining her urge to clear the sink, before she finally asked, "I assume you are not doing the dishes tonight?" Annoyed by Ellen's nudging, Dina wondered whether for once in their ten years of living together Ellen could just trust her and wait. Assuming a bit of logic would be useful at that point, she responded, "Why would I do them tonight when I can do them with tomorrow's breakfast dishes?" This was unacceptable to Ellen, who then cleared the sink because, she explained, "I worried about having huge insomnia if I went to bed with the kitchen in a mess."

You may have concluded that Dina should have considered Ellen's wishes and just taken a few minutes to wash the damned dishes. However, it is equally plausible you would think Ellen should have understood Dina's way of doing things, get over it, and go to sleep. If deadline-driven procrastinators tend to delay and task-driven people have a difficult time waiting, then they are bound to have conflict unless each partner understands the other's motivational style and negotiates responsibilities with that in mind.

Generally, people are somewhat able to adapt their partner's style in such situations. Nevertheless, what motivates you to get something done is difficult to alter at a basic emotional level. On a cognitive level, we can take the needs and values of others into consideration and even act on them (that is, adapt our style in these situations to avoid conflict) when task-completion differences affect a partnership. In fact, avoidance of a negative emotion being triggered by an unhappy partner is often enough to motivate someone in Dina's position to do the dishes sooner or, in Ellen's position, to trust that Dina will eventually wash them. At the same time, anger may be triggered in someone who feels pressured by his or her partner to do the dishes when he or she would rather wait until later and sees no negative consequences to his or her decision.

When partners have divergent styles, joint undertakings can be challenging, such as running a household or taking on a project. It does not seem to occur to those who are deadline driven that pleasurable relief for a task-driven partner has to do with completing tasks any more than it occurs to task-driven people that a procrastinator is motivated by deadlines. However, you can better navigate through a relationship with a partner who has a divergent motivational style, as well as learn from him or her, if you are able to step back, evaluate what you feel, endure the discomfort of any emotion you might be experiencing, and refrain from shaming a partner in response.

Dante and Carina provide such an example in describing an interaction following their move into a new home. Task-driven Carina suggested to deadline-driven Dante that they replace the unappealing strip of lawn in front of the house with flowers. Interpreting his response "I'll think about it" as affirmation, the following day she returned home from errands with her car packed full of 125 primroses. Emerging from the house, Dante was aghast at the sight. He reflected, "Although I didn't think she was serious, I should have known better. What I consider as an idea, for her, is something she wants to get done right now. She is such a do-it-now person."

Following an argument during which time the plants were repacked into the car, Carina drove off to the garden center crying. She considered ending their relationship so she wouldn't have to be limited by Dante's hesitation to act. Even so, Carina later recognized that she had lashed out at Dante because she had felt humiliated. When she returned home, she talked it over with him, and during their conversation, she realized that she had not considered all the factors, including how Dante really felt about replacing the lawn with primroses. She also reflected more thoughtfully about whether it had been a good idea in the first place and concluded that it was not a good idea after all when Dante had pointed out that people getting in and out of their cars would eventually trample and destroy the flowers.

GROUP PROJECTS AND DIVERGENT STYLES

Conflicts between task-driven and deadline-driven people become apparent early in life, and unfortunate rifts—and even ruptures—can result from the failure to understand one another. Imagine you are still in middle school and have been assigned to a group project along with Jeremy, Lila, and Marissa. You are all excellent students; however, you and Jeremy tend to procrastinate, whereas Lila and Marissa are task driven.

Lila and Marissa complete their part of the project early and then immediately become anxious and then critical that you and Jeremy have not done your part, even though there is still plenty of time before the project is due. Since this is a group project their task-driven focus is on your uncompleted part of the work. Lila and Marissa may even be inclined to complete your share of the project because they do not trust you'll do it or because they doubt your ability to pull it off. After all, their grade hinges on your performance as well, and they do not understand your motivational style. They may even complain to the teacher that they have done all the work and don't want you in their group or to share their grade. In any case, your relationship with them will inevitably become compromised. If your teacher doesn't understand how you get things done, then your relationship with your teacher may also be negatively affected and your own grade jeopardized. However, this bad situation can become even worse. Suppose Lila and Marissa complain to their parents about the "terrible" group members who make them do all the work. Naturally, in support of Lila and Marissa, and especially if their parents are task driven, you might be resented, and they may question the values your parents taught you. If they see your parents in a social situation and give credibility to all of the erroneous assumptions about you, they may be hesitant to have anything to do with them. Unfortunately, what seems like far-reaching and negative assumptions are not uncommon, and what's even more unfortunate is that some researchers promote them.

In a study of students' perceptions of group projects, researchers found that those students who worked with a "slacker" (the researchers' terminology) were more likely to say they did most of the work and less likely to look forward to future projects and they were also less likely to agree that they learned from members of their group.[5] One of the strategies used to motivate the slackers to get to work on their part of the project, the researchers noted, was to provide the option of "divorcing" a group member who does not contribute to the project.[6]

As you might imagine, those students who have a tendency to complete their work close to the deadline would be unfairly targeted by this divorce strategy. Moreover, a primary concern I have about the strategy has to do with the toxic effects of shaming deadline-driven students as well as shaming low achievers. Further, promoting the notion to young people that relationships are disposable rather than something to navigate, understand, and learn from is not a healthy message to convey. As discussed in Chapter 5, one cannot assume there is a connection between students who procrastinate and students who fail. Those who fail to meet deadlines do so for any number of reasons or circumstances, including cognitive and psychological issues. Procrastination is not the problem that needs to be addressed here.

In both educational and employment settings, recognizing stylistic differences in task completion could allow group members to strategize, organize, and find creative solutions to handling project completion. In fact, group projects in educational settings offer an ideal opportunity for teachers to point out differences in motivational styles and ways to discuss and navigate such variances and help their students understand that meeting deadlines and doing one's best work are essential for present and future success. One creative solution to working with students with different motivational styles would be to create markers or intermediate deadlines for portions of a group project, rather than assigning only a final project deadline, as a means of being responsive to students with both task-completion styles. Similarly, in work settings, managers who involve their employees in weekly goal assessment and performance check-ins, rather than reviewing their work performance only once or twice a year, are taking both task-completion styles into consideration. This approach is discussed further in Chapter 8.

All groups are negatively affected when some members fail to do their share of the work prior to a deadline. Invariably, those who procrastinate stand out as potential perpetrators and may be the recipients of negative perceptions on the part of their instructors as well as fellow students who are task driven. In a study where group members were interviewed regarding their recommendations for "dealing with slackers" (once again, the researcher's terminology), many participants reported an interest in confronting the slacker rather than continuing to complete the work themselves.[7] Among the confrontations for the so-called slacker, the participants suggested initial warnings, including somewhat hostile attacks, providing friendly reminders, and using non-verbal cues. However, some participants preferred to avoid conflict by doing the slacker's work themselves rather than waiting to see whether the individual would complete his or her portion of the work before the deadline.

We already know that doing the work oneself is a typical solution of task-driven partners who do not have confidence that their deadline-driven partners will do their part. However, we must not forget that procrastinators avoid conflict with nonprocrastinators as well, for example, by rewriting a coworker's suboptimal report (and it may have been suboptimal because the task-driven coworker was more focused on completing the task than taking the time to do his or her best work). Further speculating on the process of working in groups, the researchers noted that slackers may contribute to the experience others have of "grouphate"—feelings of dread about the possibility of having to work in a group.[8] It is important to keep in mind that studies such as this one do not explore the vast difference between people who fail to complete tasks and those who complete them near the deadline, nor do they take into account divergent motivational styles in general. Nevertheless, if grouphate is a possible outcome, how crucial it is to inform educators and managers about group dynamics involving people with diverse styles of task completion!

EMOTIONAL STATES AND THEIR IMPACT ON INTIMATE AND WORK RELATIONSHIPS

In the process of task completion, both task-driven or deadline-driven people may experience heightened negative emotional states and associated negative cognitions. Fear, dread, anguish, or agitation can manifest in any number of images, especially those having to do with failing. These scenarios often involve other people who, upon witnessing this stress, interpret the expressed negative emotion as a plea for comfort or even as a request for permission to abandon the task.

When task-driven Caroline is in the tumult of getting things done, for example, she claims she dislikes interruption and is easily agitated. "For some reason," she explained, "I need to be left alone and don't want anyone asking me questions or commenting on what I'm doing. I have an edge even though I may be perfectly happy in my own world. But when I see other things to do as I complete the work, I become irritable, even if it's stuff that is not a big deal if left alone. It's just that I can't stand to let anything go, so it's on me."

In contrast, Eric discussed the response of Maria, his task-driven partner, to his procrastination. He recounted that the focus, frenzy, and agitation that he experiences when striving to complete a task near the deadline annoy and worry Maria. She remarked, "At those times, there are everyday things I want him to do, but he is single focused and hyped up. Sometimes I worry about him, but he won't let me help." Eric concurred, stating, "Yes, when I am focused on finishing something at a deadline, you could drive a semitruck through the room and I wouldn't notice."

Negative emotional states that people who procrastinate experience have been the subject of wide speculation by researchers. They wonder whether procrastinators are more inclined than nonprocrastinators to experience agitation and dejection or maladjustment related to anxiety and depression.[9] [10] At the same time, however, researchers have almost completely ignored similar emotional states and possible pathology experienced by those who are compelled to complete tasks early. Even though research regarding compulsive behaviors touches on these issues, the focus is on pathology rather than normal variants of early task-completion behavior.

TRIGGERING NEGATIVE EMOTION IN BYSTANDERS

If you are in the vicinity of someone who has a motivational style that differs from your own, you may misinterpret the intense emotion he or she experiences in completing a task. Often, bystanders assume that when someone else is stressed out or seems overwhelmed by a task, his or her behavior is a plea for assistance. In fact, his or her distress and anxiety, which often pose as agitation or irritation, can trigger feelings of helplessness or guilt in those who witness it.

Emotions can be contagious to both family members and coworkers. Simply stated, you may take on as your own the emotion of another person. When emotions are transmitted to one person from another (e.g., feeling depressed when around a depressed partner) or when they are acted out on others (e.g., a sense of inadequacy about oneself expressed as a snippy response to a coworker, who in response feels inadequate), the experience is regarded as *affect contagion*.[11] This contagion can be pleasurable, such as experiencing joy when you smile at a young child, who in turn experiences joy in smiling back at you.[12] However, in a situation where a task-driven person is in a state of distress trying to get something done or when a procrastinator is fearing failure as he or she frantically completes a task as a deadline approaches, by just being in the vicinity you may take on his or her feelings, or he or she may simply impose on you what he or she feels.

If your partner or coworker has a motivational style that differs from your own, you may occasionally have a difficult time tolerating the emotion emanating from him or her. You may even experience the emotion yourself. Yet for those partners giving off that emotion, they may be so pumped up and consumed that they don't notice how others around them are being affected. If they do notice, it's probably because the other person has emphatically vocalized his or her feelings of distress or anger.

It is not a problem when we are affected by emotional messages transmitted from another person when they are highly pleasurable, such as the contagious quality of laughter or getting caught up in a partner's sexual excitement. However, when the emotional message being transmitted is not pleasurable, you will want immunity to emotional contagion and, thus, will try to find a way to block the transmission. Through learning to monitor your experience of an emotion and determining whether an emotion is generated from within yourself or from without, you will be better able to maintain your stability around another person's intense emotional experiences. Simple solutions would be to distract yourself away from the feelings you are experiencing, leave the vicinity of the person who is affecting you, or state your confidence that he or she will complete the task well as has been the case in similar situations in the past. In Chapter 2 you met Melissa and Sam, a couple who were invited to participate in a ceremony. Melissa recognized that Sam's frenzy of activity at the deadline was going to be upsetting to her, so she left their hotel room, took a walk, and thereby shielded herself from experiencing Sam's heightened emotional state as well as avoided conflict that would likely have occurred between them.

DISCONNECTION, DISRUPTION, AND SHAME RESPONSES

Commonly, we interpret the actions of others based on memories of similar experiences or situations that we have encountered in our lives. As a result, the behavior of someone with a motivational style different from our own can result in a shame response. As discussed in Chapter 5, in the context of a bond with another person, a shame response informs you that for the moment you have experienced an impediment to the maintenance of that bond.[13] Thus, what we often refer to as "hurt feelings" is caused by the emotion of shame in response to situations where the resonance between two people has been broken.[14] We can appreciate that people who get things done ahead of time have to wait for the person who procrastinates, but we should also bear in mind that people who procrastinate often have to wait for the person who is compelled to get something done right now. And when another person leaves you waiting, it's likely that shame will be activated along with one or more of the typical defensive responses to it. As a reminder, we learned in Chapter 5 that defensive responses to shame include withdrawal, avoidance, and attacking oneself or others and these responses are formed and influenced by the individual's cultural and social practices.[15]

In fact, even mundane interactions between task-driven and deadline-driven people may result in shame responses because of their differences. Shannon provided one such situation. She was excited by the possibility of attending an event that was happening in a few weeks, so she called her boyfriend, Lucas, to ask whether he would be interested in going to the event with her. In his familiar deadline-driven style, Lucas told her he would let her know. Shannon was already chagrined because Lucas was unavailable the entire day since he had chosen that particular day to finish a project that she knew he could have finished much earlier. Thus, she was primed to have a shame response to her perceived disconnection from Lucas, and in fact, she had several defensive shame responses. In a harsh tone, she attacked Lucas, exclaiming, "What's there to think about?" Starting to cry, she then attacked herself, telling him, "If you really wanted to be with me, then the decision wouldn't need much thought." Shannon then hung up on Lucas and in that moment made a pact with herself that she would not contact him for the rest of the week.

Now, of course, procrastinators don't delay about everything, so in this situation, it's possible that if Lucas had been as excited as Shannon was about the event, he may have been motivated to buy tickets immediately. Was Lucas stalling because he didn't want to go, or did he really want to think about it, perhaps weighing the possibility alongside other activities they could do that weekend? Most likely, Lucas was driven by a deadline, and, highly focused on completing the task he was working on, he did not want to interrupt his process. In any case, as Shannon and Lucas demonstrated, task-driven partners may not recognize that deadline-driven people often *do* prefer to think about things. Similarly, deadline-driven partners may not understand how their response may affect a task-driven partner who expects a rapid decision or immediate action. Typically, procrastinators might say that waiting gives them more time to think about things and has nothing to do with their feelings about the other person. However, even if Shannon doesn't take her partner's delay personally, the pending decision will bother her until it's made. Her own feelings of shame might even lead her to shame her partner with repeated inquiries. The situation may have been helped if Lucas had told Shannon he'd really enjoy doing something with her but he needed a couple of hours to consider the possibility of going to the event *after* his project was finished. Similarly, Shannon could have asked him to call and let her know within two hours following the deadline for his project. Either situation would represent a deadline for Lucas and interim relief for Shannon. Instead, feelings were hurt, assumptions were made, and communication was limited until a lot of unnecessary damage was done. Shame doesn't tell us to respond defensively in any of those typical ways. Instead, it informs us of our internal perception of what's going on. Embroiled in her disconnection and hurt, Shannon did not tell Lucas what she was feeling.

Deadline-driven people, in their interactions with task-driven partners, also experience shame. Meghan, for example, described feeling slighted whenever her task-driven partner would interrupt their conversations to check his ringing phone to see who was calling or look at his e-mail whenever he would hear the alerting sound of an incoming message. These interruptions occurred anywhere, whether they were sitting in a restaurant, watching a movie at home, or walking down the street. Sometimes Meghan would angrily accuse her partner of being weird, disrespectful, or compulsive, and at other moments she wondered whether she was not enough for him to pay attention to her rather than check his phone. His response was always the same: he does it so that it's not on his mind. Eventually, she let him know that she felt humiliated and alone at those times.

How we deal with shame when we experience it and the ways in which we respond to others who experience shame in relation to us are critical to healthy learning and our ability to interact socially and intimately.[16] Defensive responses to shame cannot be characterized as either bad or good. They simply serve to help you cope with what you feel. If at the moment you do not have the emotional resources to face how you are feeling, avoidance or withdrawal may be what you need. Distancing yourself from the problem may help with your stability until you are able to take a look at the issues you face and better define them in such a way that you will be able to repair and strengthen your connections with others. Healthy responses to shame include addressing the shame, searching the situation with interest to find out what triggered it, and then reflecting on and deciding what to do in response.

When shame is experienced in a work or group setting of any kind, it can damage feelings of belonging and the formation of community. If shame can interfere with feelings of community, then strengthening the community by talking openly and candidly about what is going on can shift attention to mutual goals. Naturally, there is an optimal level of emotional safety that must be reached to do so. Understanding, engagement, and interaction can counterbalance the negative judgments and powerlessness so often associated with shame.

Emotions not only give you information and motivation, but in addition, they are your teachers. Shame is a profound teacher since often it draws you within yourself to think deeply about yourself in relation to others.[17] A personal connection with others is the vehicle that helps people develop an ability to tolerate distress and dissolve shame and learn what the connection can convey.

In sum, divergent task-completion styles often present challenges to intimate and work relationships. The central focus of both task-driven and deadline-driven people should be to evaluate the task-completion situations in terms of meeting deadlines and putting one's best efforts into the work. Agitation and annoyance are commonly experienced toward others who have a motivational style that differs from your own. In the workplace as well as in intimate relationships, it is important to recognize the impact of another person's behavior on you and address situations of conflict with interest rather than with shaming the other person or yourself.

Recognizing that everyone can improve on how they get things done, the next chapter is devoted to the ways in which you can optimize your motivational style. I won't try to change you but, hopefully, just make you better at what you already do in terms of completing tasks.

Chapter 8

OPTIMIZING YOUR MOTIVATIONAL STYLE

A lifetime of learning has determined how you get things done. Therefore, I wouldn't dream of suggesting you change what has worked for you. Instead, let's find ways to upgrade your motivational style. We are always capable of learning in response to our emotions and through exploring our reactions to emotions. First of all, let's not get caught up defending the way we get things done. People have differences, and those variances are often based on many years of emotional experiences. The more productive approach is to evaluate outcome. Do you get things done and do them well? If so, that's a good place to begin. Nonetheless, you may have misinterpreted as pathological the emotions that get you to a successful place. By now, hopefully, you better understand the emotions that motivate you. The trick is to interpret and use them wisely.

For those who have been failing at task completion, there is likely plenty of shame you've had to hide from yourself and others. Consider this shame as information that you have not met the higher standard you had set for yourself. Take a genuine look at what may have contributed to any failure you've experienced. It's imperative that you not blame a failure to meet deadlines on procrastinating or attribute your lack of progress to your need to put tasks behind you and thus do suboptimal work. Because such excuses often hide shame, what's really getting in the way remains hidden as well. I invite you to take a few steps toward success. Hindsight may offer you more insight than what you can gain by trying to examine yourself only while your boat is sinking. Aside from that, you must remember that your goal is to create new emotional memories of success that will supersede your memories of failure. In the event that you need some prompting toward a successful approach, finding mentors who align with your motivational style, but who do it right, can really help. Perhaps you will be able to identify with some of the examples included in this chapter. Even so, I understand that it's not always easy to pull yourself up and alter a deeply engrained pattern.

EMBRACING YOUR TASK-COMPLETION STYLE

If you procrastinate, you may have experienced what happens when you attempt to get something done long before its deadline. From an emotional perspective, you may not be motivated to attend to a specific task until you have become anxious about it or fear you will fail, which invariably will be close to the deadline. At this point, the task activates emotions that are intense enough to harness your attention. Occasionally, procrastinators are motivated to do things on the early side, as discussed in Chapter 2. These circumstances may involve a specific request made by someone of import to you, avoiding a partner's or employer's displeasure, or financial considerations or safety or health issues.

Typically, deadline-driven procrastinators find it unnecessary, not useful, and even impossible to alter their approach to tasks, which is one reason I'd be self-defeating if I tried to change you. However, you can learn about yourself if you pay attention to what goes on during the process of working on something. Consider Anthony, for example, who noted, "When I try to do something in advance, my thoughts just aren't there. I can't do it." Describing his typical process of procrastinating, he said, "When a deadline is in sight, everything seems to come together in my head. I put it down on paper, and that's it. I can always be trusted to deliver an excellent product on time." Since his livelihood involves writing a lot of reports, Anthony makes sure that everyone who requests them either already knows or is told that he wants an absolute deadline.

However, one day as Anthony was thinking about the next report he had to complete, he began experiencing his usual fear of failure. His thought led him to wonder whether he was being arrogant in not re-viewing his documents before sending them out. The thought that his reports may have been less than excellent and that he should have been reviewing them along the way made him anxious and very motivated to seek confirmation. Arbitrarily, he opened files and read reports that he had written in the past five years. He found nothing he would have altered. Even so, Anthony's own assessment of his previous work was not enough to relieve his shame anxiety. Therefore, he offered to pay two colleagues who were familiar with these types of reports to critique a few of his own that he had randomly chosen. When both reviewers highly praised the reports and had no suggestions for improvement, Anthony then began to wonder why he had doubted himself in the first place but saved his musings for later since now the deadline was immi-nent to write his current report. Actually, it is not unusual for procrasti-nators to doubt themselves when they are in the midst of shame anxiety about a specific task they must finish. Thus, on the day Anthony started doubting the accuracy of his reports, an approaching deadline had trig-gered shame anxiety, which he placed in the context of a fear of failure about his work in general rather than on the specific task at hand.

Like Anthony, many professionally successful procrastinators re-quest that deadlines be created in circumstances that do not have defi-nite cutoff points. In situations wherein deadlines are unclear or not externally determined, procrastinators use various other maneuvers to create them. A typical example is to set a timer to a certain interval, such as thirty minutes, and then challenge oneself to complete various tasks within that chosen period of time. Some procrastinators tell an-other person about their target date for a project as a commitment incentive. If people ask you to give them a deadline, they need one. Do them a favor and not only give them a deadline but tell them to check in with you on that date or at that time. Another strategy is to schedule the task around other work or activities, as this gives some procrastinators the sense of less available time to get a task done. If you are successful as a procrastinator, you likely have your own set of tricks to create deadlines when they do not otherwise exist.

For task-driven people, waiting until a deadline is near may activate emotions to such intense levels that they will be disruptive and interfere with their ability to focus. Waiting until a deadline is near may also cut into the time ordinarily used to review one's work, causing worry and greater anxiety. Claudia, whose career also involves writing reports, observed that her style of doing things in advance allows her time to revise reports numerous times, and on occasion, she will reverse her decisions or conclusions. She lamented, "Sometimes when I have time to review and obsess, I work it so much that I'm afraid I take the life out of it even though people seem to love my reports." She theorized that she could reduce the time she seemed to require, as well as limit her obsessing while maintaining her creativity, if she waited to write a report until a deadline was close. She found that she was nearly out of her mind with anxiety, and it was even harder for her to think or make decisions on what to write. Looking back, Claudia explained, "I felt so pressured that I almost humiliated myself and risked my reputation by asking for more time, but it wouldn't have helped. I'll never do that to myself again."

There is likely a temporal point at which you perform optimally in terms of task completion. Although tasks can get completed another way, there may be obstacles to overcome, such as limited motivation for procrastinators or deadline distress if you are task driven. Given your motivational style, you have to determine what works best for you, be secure that you will complete what has to get done, and know that you have put your best efforts into the task. I cannot stress enough that learning how you learn and get things done is important in this regard. Step back from any situation and take a look at what you do.

The ability to alter your motivational style, if the situation requires it or for other external reasons, does not mean that you will always have the emotional resources available to easily tackle a task. A good analogy is provided by how we once regarded handedness. In the past, left-handedness was negatively viewed, just as procrastination is negatively regarded at the present time. Previously, people assumed that left-handedness was voluntary, unnecessary, and even evidence of a sinful nature.[1] We still do not fully understand the neuropsychological issues involved in hand dominance, nor do we fully understand why task-driven and deadline-driven people respond differently to the biological system that produces emotions. Perhaps as neuroscientists come to better understand how emotions bias attention, as well as why some people show differences in working memory and are predisposed to attend to certain categories of emotionally important stimuli over others, we may better comprehend why some tend to procrastinate and others do not. In any case, if you wish to optimize your motivational style, you must first identify what it is and wholeheartedly embrace it rather than focus on how to change it or mull over why change seems impossible to do.

RESPONDING TO INTENSE EMOTION

Many people feel disrupted by their emotions in response to tasks. Deadline-driven procrastinators may feel unsettled along with, or in response to, the intense emotion they experience at a deadline. In their own way, task-driven people become flustered if they interpret the activation of emotion in response to any uncompleted task as a mandate to take action, as though something bad might happen if they do not attend to it right away. When a biologically based emotion is triggered by a stimulus—such as a task to complete—and produces a response, our cognitive system takes into account all of our prior experiences when that emotion was activated and informs us to react in a particular way. The space between our emotional response and how we react to it is a place where we can make adjustments that optimize our approach to tasks. Thus, when you feel intense emotion, take a moment to consider what the emotions is telling you rather than quickly react to what you feel. Consider, for example what the feelings in your body are motivating you to do. The thoughts that accompany those feelings are your attempt, based on past experience, to focus those feelings. However, this time pay attention to what you feel rather than count solely on past experience.

Deadline-driven Anna, for example, explained that she used to become terribly upset when the deadline for something was close. She would cry, scream, fall into despair, and tear herself up inside. Denigrating herself, she was certain she was going to fail because she was a "loser" who procrastinated, even though she was highly successful in her career. She has no recall of what changed in her, except for sitting with her feelings and realizing that they got her moving. Subsequently, as she felt the tension come up, she said to herself instead, "Okay, this is it, so let's get going." Since that time, she hasn't put such a negative spin on completing a task when the deadline is near. In her words, "I just sort of listen to my feelings and tell myself it must be time to do whatever I have to do because they are so intense. Then I tell myself to get it done."

At such moments, prior to starting to work on a task, some procrastinators imagine anxiety-laden scenarios involving potential failure. Even when people are comfortable and secure with a deadline-driven style and look forward to the "rush" experienced when racing the clock, they are not without some negative emotion and corresponding thoughts. Thus, it is important to recognize that these negative feelings and thoughts will dissolve as you attend to the task. Unfortunately, people who fail sometimes are so overfocused on a debilitating negative image that they give up rather than apply the energy produced by their emotion to attend to the task at hand.

Task-driven people are inclined to interpret emotion activation as a mandate to take action, as though any task that activates some distress cannot be disregarded. Lindsey, for instance, described the enormous stress she experienced as a result of having numerous things to do between her work and family. She couldn't let things go and wasn't able to wait when any little task came to her attention. Eventually, she learned to recognize that when she felt compelled to get something done, she could either do it or place limits on her unremitting motivation to complete tasks right away. Although emotions will motivate you to take action, especially if you are a task-driven person such as Lindsey, you must carefully evaluate the importance or necessity of taking action immediately. Rather than interpret her intense emotions as an obligation to attend to something immediately, Lindsey instead began to reassure and remind herself "It's not the time to do this," or "I don't have to do this right now," or "It won't matter to anyone if this is done or not." Giving such consideration to what she feels and thinks, rather than instantly reacting to it, reminds her that she has a choice about when to take care of the items on her to-do list or what she notices that "should" be done right now.

Both Anna and Lindsey present vivid examples of paying attention to what their emotions are telling them, taking a look at the thoughts that accompany what they feel, and then evaluating the information their emotions provide. In an interpersonal situation, for example, when another person suggests where you should focus your attention and what you should do, hopefully you will be able to evaluate whether the recommendation is in your best interest. It's no different with emotions and accompanying thoughts that are activated by a task. They exist to inform you along with the judgment of your cognitive system, but the action you take, to a great extent, is under your own control.

Reappraising Anxiety and Distress Arousal

If you are success oriented, you've probably noticed how familiar you are with stress. Perhaps your partner or coworkers occasionally suggest that you calm down. Generally, logic and self-help guidelines recommend that you should learn to manage states of high arousal from stress. However, keep in mind what was noted in Chapter 3: physiological arousal during stressful tasks is adaptive and serves an important purpose. So before you calm yourself down too much—whether with deep breathing, relaxing thoughts, alcohol, drugs, or anything else—evaluate how your stress might help you, which I explain shortly.

Nevertheless, there are situations where you may be best served by cognitively reframing or reappraising your situation or what you are feeling at the moment to calm yourself. The reasoning behind this approach is that thinking differently about what you are feeling or the situation at hand helps you to attain composure. Similarly, the suggestions above for procrastinators and task-driven people to work with and consider their emotions are a form of reappraisal. Importantly, reframing or reappraisal does not necessarily imply that anxiety and distress represent something that is going wrong in your body, rather than right, in response to a situation.

One technique that is suggested for managing stress is to reappraise anxiety, a negative emotion, as excitement, a positive emotion, which can help you make good use of emotion rather than attempt to rid yourself of it. Thus, instead of trying to suppress what you feel and calm yourself down, reappraising anxiety as excitement may enhance performance and contribute to an elevated mood.[2] Anxiety and excitement are arousal congruent; that is, both are felt in anticipation of events and characterized by high arousal.[3] Feeling more excited and adopting an opportunity mindset, as opposed to a mindset involving threat, can be achieved by using minimal strategies such as self-talk (one researcher, for example, suggests saying, "I'm excited" out loud) or simple messages (such as telling yourself to "get excited").[4] In a study that used the contexts of singing, public speaking, and math, the researchers found that people who reappraised anxiety as excitement, compared to those who reappraised anxiety as calmness or not reappraising it at all, improved their performance.[5] Interpreting your anxiety as excitement, as opposed to calming yourself, will preserve the motivation provided by the emotion, yet such successful reappraisal is not always possible to achieve.

In terms of optimizing your approach to task completion, reappraising arousal in a manner in which you accept what you feel, rather than reframing it as another emotion, may help you recognize and employ it as adaptive and useful. A study conducted at Harvard University found that participants who positively reappraised arousal—considering physiological arousal during a stressful task as functional and adaptive—exhibited more adaptive cardiovascular stress responses, increased cardiac efficiency and decreased vascular resistance, and decreased attentional bias.[6] For example, the butterflies you feel in your chest or stomach when you are about to perform may represent a fear of the unknown or a fear of failure (shame anxiety). If your goal is to get rid of the feeling or view it as threatening, you are more likely to experience distraction and frustration. Instead, if you adopt the mindset that physical symptoms of arousal are a signal that your body is energized or preparing you to meet a challenge, they can, in fact, maximize your performance.[7] Thus, when you feel the sensation of butterflies, accept it as your body's way of responding to a challenge in the same way you use bodily sensations that alert you in a truly threatening situation.

Similarly, how you perceive your experience of stress has an impact on your health. Successful task-driven people tend to see themselves as continuously stressed, and procrastinators are often highly aware of feeling stressed when a deadline is upon them. Yet although they may go so far as to think of themselves as "neurotic," they do not necessarily view their stress negatively. Instead, stress is often perceived as energy that enables them to get things done. A study based on the National Health Interview Survey of over 28,000 adults examined whether the perception that stress affects health matters in later health and mortality rates.[8] High levels of stress coupled with the perception that stress affects health were associated with an increased likelihood of worse mental health and physical health outcomes, as well as a 43 percent increased risk of premature death, whereas those who did not believe that stress was harmful had the lowest risk of dying of anyone in the study.

Task Completion and Sleep

There are times when your style of getting things done might compromise your sleep. Whether you are task driven or deadline driven, compromised sleep habits are an indication that you have not optimized your task-completion style. Proper sleep habits are essential for many reasons. Likely, you are already aware of the negative impact of irregular or disrupted sleep.

During the years of their formal education, some procrastinators fall into the habit of staying up all night to complete tasks. Task-driven people develop a habit of staying awake at night worrying about unfinished tasks so they will not forget to do them. Worse yet, they may remain awake attending to a task that can wait, as though it has to be done now. For the most part, professionally successful people recognize that sleep is a high priority. They structure their lives in a way that maintains a healthy sleep schedule.

If you are not getting enough sleep as a deadline-driven person, you must reevaluate the timing of deadlines in a way that takes into consideration how essential it is to get enough restorative sleep. If you are task driven, you must assess whether any task is critical enough for your sleep to be compromised or trust that you will complete the task in a given time frame the following day. In any case, if you are unable to make adjustments so you are not losing sleep, you may want to consult a specialist to guide you. Rather than belabor the point, I'll simply say, rather emphatically, that your task-completion style should never interfere with a normal and regular sleep pattern. If it does interfere, you are compromising yourself and your well-being, so please make adjustments.

INTENSE EMOTION AND TASK-COMPLETION INTERFERENCE

As a deadline approaches, procrastinators may entertain the possibility of getting a deadline extension. The counterpart in task-driven people is the possibility of somehow escaping the situation. However, as noted in Chapter 2, these are fleeting images that arise with the emotion that is felt at the time. Successful people rarely extend a deadline or withdraw from a project, even though it may cross their minds. A task-driven financial consultant described this process around a presentation she was to deliver at the corporate headquarters of a client. She imagined being relieved of the task by circumstances beyond her control—illness, an earthquake, or a broken leg. However, once she was well into the work she needed to do as preparation, the images vanished.

You might save yourself time and mental energy by recognizing extension and escape fantasies as fleeting cognitions. They are in response to emotion that you automatically interpreted as a vague threat. Thus, your brain provides you with images and suggestions to help you alter the situation or circumstance. On a daily basis, you encounter numerous situations when emotions are activated and your brain creates corresponding images. Your action or inaction often is based on an instantaneous assessment of what the emotion is telling you relative to what's going on around you and the images you create. So optimize your motivational style by just sitting with the images for a minute, and recognize that your creative mind is forming a scenario that corresponds with whatever emotion you are feeling at the time. Acknowledge the emotion, and remind yourself that it is just trying to help motivate and prepare you for action.

COMMITMENT TO GOALS

Professionally successful people are emotionally attached to their goals. Keeping promises to yourself regarding your achievement aims is an important aspect of optimizing your motivational style. To-do lists are popular for a variety of reasons, and successful people use them as a way to commit to completing a task now or later. One procrastinator described creating a list of tasks every evening, along with a commitment to himself that he would complete them the following day. In this way, he imposed a deadline for those tasks; those lists, for him, represent commitments he makes and keeps.

Lists made by task-driven people are also regarded as commitments; however, they do not serve as self-imposed deadlines as they do for procrastinators. Instead, a list focuses the task-driven person's attention on defined tasks to complete and limits the distraction of anything else that might instead garner his or her attention. Because they are so prone to complete tasks early, task-driven people are also fearful of forgetting what has to get done. One task-driven person described her list of to-do items as a way to keep some things just hanging so she wouldn't feel so crazed about having to do everything all at once. Her to-do list keeps her from constantly thinking about them so she will not forget.

OPTIMAL MANAGEMENT OF MOTIVATIONAL STYLES IN THE WORKPLACE

Great managers don't try to change their employees, but instead, they identify their employees' unique abilities, recognize their diverse learning and implementation styles, and help them use those qualities to excel in their own way.[9] The eminent management consultant and researcher Marcus Buckingham divides learning styles into realms of analyzers, doers, and watchers. Like procrastinators, analyzers take their time to absorb information about a subject before they move on. They prepare diligently to minimize the possibility of errors, and their most powerful learning moments occur prior to the performance. In contrast, the most powerful moments for doers, much like task-driven people, occur during their performance since their learning process involves trial and error. Doers learn the most while in the act of figuring things out for themselves, and mistakes are the raw material for their learning. Watchers, on the other hand, do not learn by doing or even by role-playing; instead, they learn best by watching an experienced performer.[10]

Similarly, it is important for managers to recognize that tasks motivate some people who report to them, but that others may be motivated by deadlines. Further, whether an employee completes a task early on or at the deadline is less important than evaluating outcome. Productivity can be increased when managers recognize motivational styles and set goals accordingly. Procrastinators and nonprocrastinators may work together best, for example, when there are short-term deadlines within a long-term project. This process artificially creates a deadline for those who need one and focuses attention on a particular task for those distracted by many other things to do. As such, this structure effectively makes use of divergent motivational styles.

In summary, human motivation is complex, and yet it always involves emotions, whether or not they are within our awareness at any given time. Thus, if you want to optimize the way you get things done, as well as the ways in which you live your life in general, I wholeheartedly endorse understanding the emotions that drive you.

Optimizing your motivational style involves clearly identifying whether you are motivated by tasks themselves or by a looming deadline, but you must also be able to identify the temporal point at which you optimally function in terms of task completion. Successful people, whether they are task-driven or deadline-driven, adopt various maneuvers that are most advantageous to their way of doing things. In any case, task completion is often accompanied by stress. You may respond negatively when you are physically aroused by stress; however, stress arousal is a tool that helps us maximize our performance. As well, healthy sleep habits are essential for optimal performance, and you may need to make adjustments if your task-completion style interferes with a normal and regular sleep pattern. A troubleshooting guide for your motivational system—a synopsis of the recommendations presented here—can be found in the next chapter.

Chapter 9

TROUBLESHOOTING GUIDE

If you are someone who prefers a summary of information rather than a narrative, this chapter offers bullet points for the content discussed in Chapter 8. You may want to use it as a review or as a compilation of strategies that pertain to your particular motivational style. The guidelines for a style that differs from your own may help you understand the challenges and strategies of others and assist you in navigating through conflicts that result from motivational style differences. These guidelines also provide information that can be used to mentor, supervise, or direct employees or students.

As you read this guide, keep in mind the central goals that lead to success: never miss a deadline, and put your best efforts into your work.

GENERAL GUIDELINES

- Learn about yourself by observing and exploring your emotional responses and reactions to emotions that are activated. Always assume you can improve on your motivational style.
- To effectively employ your motivational system, understand the emotions that drive you, and recognize the thoughts that arise along with them.
- Recognize the space between your emotional response and reaction to what you feel. Adapt your reaction according to your ultimate

goals, recognizing that you have learned to react in specific ways to what you feel.

- Appreciate that you are motivated both to feel the good effects of positive emotions and avoid or relieve the effects of negative emotions.
- Observe how your motivational style contributes to how you operate in the world and the ways in which it affects your interactions with others.
- Make note of when you perform optimally. Consider circumstances when you have been particularly effective, and use them as a frame of reference.
- Respond with interest and curiosity, rather than defensively, if you are criticized by another person regarding your style. Find out how your style affects them and navigate through the conflict.
- Learn from mistakes.
- Be committed to your goals and keep promises to yourself regarding what you must accomplish to get you there.

TROUBLESHOOTING A DEADLINE-DRIVEN STYLE

Minimal Motivational Thrust (Requiring a Deadline to Jump-Start Your System)

- Request a deadline or create one yourself in circumstances that do not have definite cutoff points.
- Use a to-do list that you resolve to get through by the end of the day, or create a list of tasks every evening, along with a commitment to yourself to complete them by a specific time the following day.
- Set a timer to a certain interval, such as thirty minutes, or commit to a specified length of time, such as several hours, and then challenge yourself to complete various tasks within that given period of time.
- Narrow the time available to complete certain tasks. Schedule a task around other work or activities, giving you less available time to get a task done. Challenge yourself to get something done prior to leaving the house for a meeting or activity. Create a time crunch by interjecting other tasks that you also want to get done within a certain time frame.

- As a commitment incentive, tell another person whose perception of you is important your target date for a project.
- Be aware of when you perform optimally.

Motivational System Is Nocturnal

- Recognize you have mistakenly learned to include your sleeping hours as available time to complete tasks. This is simply something you learned that is not adaptive in the long run. Your bedtime is a deadline you must always try to meet. If you are missing sleep to get something done, a temporal adjustment should be made for your future deadlines.
- Do not allow yourself anything less than healthy sleep habits. Make a commitment to yourself that all deadlines must take into consideration your sleep schedule by structuring your life and the completion of tasks accordingly.
- Check your caffeine level. If it is high, then you need to make adjustments that will lower them.

When Images Appear on Your Mental Screen Having to Do with Extensions

- Do not take seriously your thoughts of extending a deadline or withdrawing from a project, even though it may cross your mind.
- Recognize extension fantasies as fleeting fantasies. Respond only with momentary interest and enjoyment, such as having a sense of humor about these comforting illusions.

Emotions Feel Stuck in High Gear

- When you are in a high level of operation, full speed ahead, you may imagine anxiety-laden scenarios that involve potential failure. Do not assign a negative value to the intense emotions you feel around a close deadline. When intense emotions emerge, view them as a signal of energy coming your way.
- As your motivation is building, be mindful of any tendency to attribute what you feel to negative or irrelevant sources, such as consider-

ing you are in the wrong career. Defer such thinking until after the task has been completed. Simply make a promise to yourself that you will reconsider your circumstances or career at that time, and accept your intense emotion as motivation to complete the task.

- Dialogue with people who live or work with you about your style, requesting they not take personally your emotional unavailability when you are immersed in completing a task.

TROUBLESHOOTING A TASK-DRIVEN STYLE

Motivation Stuck in Urgent Mode

- Be aware of interpreting emotion activation as a mandate to take action, as though any task that activates anxiety or distress cannot be disregarded. Evaluate the importance or necessity of taking action immediately. When appropriate for the situation, consider telling yourself "It's not the time to do this," or "I don't have to do this right now," or "It won't matter to anyone if this is done or not."
- Be mindful of times when you may benefit from greater flexibility or deferring task completion until later.
- Do not send off a document until you are certain it is the final one. If you find yourself repeatedly changing documents after you've already sent them off, remind yourself that you have more time to sit with your work, and set a time for the final version to be sent.
- Create a to-do list as a way to commit to completing a task now or later. This can quell your urgency to complete tasks, as it can serve as reassurance that you will not forget to do something. Lists can also focus your attention on defined tasks to complete, limiting the distraction of everything else.

Emotions Feel Stuck in High Gear

- Do not assign a negative value to your intense emotions. They may be diverting your focus to uncompleted tasks, or they are trying to give you the energy it will take to get all of them done. Cognitively, evaluate the situation and determine whether some things can wait until another time. Write them on a list so you do not have to be concerned about forgetting them. Then reassure yourself that you will either get to the tasks later or that it will be fine if you leave them unfinished.

- Stay away from close deadlines if you become unable to do your best work when highly pressured in terms of time. However, be aware that by giving yourself too much time you may become unhinged in making revisions to your work and have to self-impose a deadline to complete the project.
- Be aware of times when others may want your attention as you are immersed in completing tasks. Trust that others will complete tasks in their own time. Dialogue with people who live or work with you about your style, requesting they not take personally your emotional unavailability.

Motivational System Is Nocturnal

- Structure your life in a way that maintains a healthy sleep schedule.
- Assess whether any task is critical enough for your sleep to be compromised.
- Reassure yourself that you will not forget about a task to complete rather than stay awake at night worrying about it.
- Make a note of the task, and assure yourself that you will take care of it the following day.
- Check your caffeine level. If your caffeine consumption is high, you will need to make adjustments to lower it.

Images Appear on Your Mental Screen Having to do with Escape

- Recognize escape fantasies as fleeting cognitions. Respond only with momentary interest and enjoyment. Find humor in your creative way of imagining getting out of something you have to do.

TROUBLESHOOTING FAILING MOTIVATION

- Determine your actual motivational style, specifically, whether you are motivated by tasks themselves or by a looming deadline. If you are unmotivated by anything and everything, consider what is getting in the way of your success, or seek professional help to discover what is interfering with your goals.
- Find mentors who successfully employ a motivational style that aligns with yours.
- Recognize and take care of any issues that may contribute to failed attempts to get things done adequately. If you are deadline driven, do not blame a failure to meet deadlines on procrastinating. If you are task driven, do not attribute your lack of progress to your need to put tasks behind you and thus tend to do suboptimal work.
- Be aware of the ways in which a failure to meet a deadline or inadequate attention to a task affects others. When you fail to get things done adequately or before a deadline passes, unintentionally you may fail others as well as yourself.
- If the motivation to realize your goals is overshadowed by personal issues, it's time to figure out what's going on with you. You may need to resolve the way you think about yourself and consider what is affecting you emotionally that handicaps your success. Every person can own success, and you can claim your space in that crowd.
- Be unafraid of what you feel. Face any shame you experience and learn from it.
- Take a few steps toward success. Be aware of the times you are motivated and what you do with the energy provided by your emotional system. Notice the thoughts that enter your mind or the feelings you have that recall past failures. Vow to create new emotional memories that involve success. Achievement can be very habit forming. Start with a little, learn from any obstacles, and see what happens.

Chapter 10

LOOKING BACK AND MOVING FORWARD

Emotional memories are powerful. They serve to guide and inform us as we navigate through the present and prepare for the future. If you've ever tasted something spoiled, you recognize one of the ways in which emotional memory protects your future decisions. Unfortunately, sometimes we unintentionally apply that same principle to relationships, such as when an emotional memory cautions us and interferes with the pursuit of having love in our life. On the other hand, sometimes our emotional memories inform us of a truth that we do not want to acknowledge, which then can lead to disregarding our feelings in order to maintain a particular belief. When a bad relationship eventually ends, for instance, often it is then safe to acknowledge what had been felt. Even so, we give credit to cognition in saying "I knew it," when actually we *felt* it long before we were willing to listen to our emotional messages.

How fortunate that the human mind can summon emotional memories of exciting and unsullied love, pride in endeavors, or joy that was felt at an amazing moment in time. Through daydreams we may muse about the past because we want to re-create a satisfying emotional experience, if only fleetingly. Although remembering an event, a situation, or a person can evoke a shiver of excitement, it can also remind us of the heat of anger or the anguish of grief. When a particular situation, thought, stimulus, or event activates an emotional memory, it can be enjoyable or painful, although it may not be felt as intensely as the original experience of the emotion. Something as simple as a particular time of year or a specific date may trigger emotional memories. Often, when a present or upcoming date coincides with the anniversary of a loss, for example, memories of the loss become consciously or preconsciously present in our minds.

Anything that is connected to our senses may be a cue that can ignite emotional recall. While visiting an Italian street fair in San Diego, California, for example, my attention became focused on a concession where two elderly Italian vendors were cooking and selling sausage sandwiches. Truly, I had no intention of eating a sausage sandwich. Even so, the delicious aroma drew me near, conjuring pleasurable childhood memories of watching my mother cook fresh salsiccia and my fondness for the scent that emanated from the grill. In essence, I became captivated as a result of olfactory memories and imagery that had been activated by the smell. Given the ability of our brains to instantaneously scan an extraordinary number of emotional memories, I also suspect that the aroma, as well as the Italian street fair generally, activated my longing for the mother I had lost early in my life—memories that ordinarily rest comfortably in the recesses of my psyche.

Nonetheless, on its own merits, the aroma of sausages on the grill that beautiful day in San Diego was very enticing. In fact, a flock of seagulls hovering low and above me were allured as well. Unexpectedly, my enchantment was interrupted when one of the seagulls pooped on my head. Clearly, the gull must have had a lot to eat at the street fair. Startle, disgust, distress, and mild shame (embarrassment) must have been apparent in my facial expression as I touched the sizeable puddle of goop in my hair and, of course, became highly motivated to do something about it. The surprised faces of the Italian men cooking sausages turned joyful as they shouted, "E buona fortuna!" (It's good luck!) and "Acquistare un biglietto della lotteria!" (Buy a lottery ticket!) Together, the three of us laughed.

One could conclude that the vendors' perception of the situation enabled me to cognitively reframe a negatively perceived event as a fortunate one; however, more than cognition was involved in the reappraisal. The emotional memories that influenced who I became are colored by many experiences of listening to elders in my Italian family, including my mother, make exuberant pronouncements based on their cultural superstitions. Prompted by the prophecies of the two men, my emotional system instantaneously scanned those memories, reevaluated the situation, and triggered joy that commingled with the surprise, disgust, distress, and shame I felt about the poop on my head. The result was laughter. If the situation had instead been reminiscent of past experiences when I had been angry or shamed, my reaction might have been different. I was indeed fortunate, as the experience echoed my positive attachments to my past.

We cannot erase emotional memories, although we can be aware of what activates them and the interpretations we make. In addition, we can alter our current reactions to past and present emotional responses. People who have been in psychotherapy, especially those who have been involved in long-term or in-depth therapy, are often alarmed that a present circumstance or stimulus activates old feelings they assumed had been worked through or extinguished. The fact is that our emotional memories serve a purpose and we really cannot pick and choose which ones we want to keep. Besides, not only can we learn extraordinary lessons from the unpleasant or painful ones, but all of our emotional memories are an important part of who we have become.

Erroneously, we sometimes assume we should do whatever we can to think positively about everything. Actually, in some situations having positive thoughts seems impossible, especially when a present situation is dreadful and negative emotions or emotional memories are working hard to inform us. When we make an effort to see the glass half full, which is what we do when we attempt to cognitively and positively reappraise a circumstance or situation that is actually pretty awful, we are trying to activate a positive emotion in a situation that triggers a negative one. Our biological system of emotions can outsmart us, however, and refuse to accept a positive reappraisal. After all, it has an advantage given its job to encode and store all of our emotional memories as well as to instantaneously retrieve them. Thus, your brain may decide it is not in your best interest to disregard what it is making you feel, along with the corresponding negative spin on what you think. As a result, you may not be able to alter a particular emotional response. Perhaps during your waking hours you can make progress in fooling your emotional system, but at night as you are trying to sleep and your guard is let down emotion will break through. Instead, however, you can evaluate your reactions to what you feel. Just as an emotion is our biological system's best guess, so are the thoughts that accompany our feelings. Being mindful of emotional responses—just sitting with them—can help us recognize their foundation in past experiences and enable us to reevaluate our reactions.

Emotions are such a neat and well-arranged system. The accumulation of emotional experiences, especially in our interactions with other people, script our present responses when a biologically based emotion is activated. These scripts organize information in our brains so we do not have to relearn the knowledge we gained from prior similar experiences. For the most part, these neat little packages of emotional memories influence our decisions and how we govern our lives. Even so, sometimes what we learn is not entirely correct, or we don't quite learn what we need to know to achieve our goals but instead respond according to old scripts. Task-completion styles or the failure to adequately complete tasks illustrates how our lifetime of responses to our innate motivational system can script our behavior in different ways. Because of repeated experiences of shame in academic situations, some children learn to avoid challenges rather than risk shame by trying and failing. This further keeps them from opportunities that will help them form new and different emotional memories.

When we simply look at behavior, without exploring what actually motivates it, we often fail to recognize the biological, psychological, and social influences that account for differences among people. In fact, we might instead criticize or shame others for their differences or for being unlike us. Similarly, numerous behaviors and convictions are subjected to negative judgment and criticism, from political party preferences to religious beliefs, although these are the result of having an ideology that is fueled by emotion. Indeed, so much of human behavior, including personality traits, can be understood by recognizing the emotions behind it.

Emotions motivate you to get things done, because they make you care: you care because you feel something. Although task-driven nonprocrastinators, along with many procrastination researchers, may perceive deadline-driven procrastinators as not caring, that's not the case. All of us, both consciously and unconsciously, are continuously caring in some way, as we are always processing information conveyed by our emotions. Sadly, even those who consistently fail to meet deadlines or do suboptimal work have emotions that make them care. However, they have learned to use coping responses to what they feel that often result in further failure.

Navigating the terrain of emotional obstacles that interfere with success is not always easy, but it certainly is possible with the help of the emotion of interest. We can approach any feeling with interest—a curiosity about the sensations we feel and the thoughts that accompany them—and accept the feeling as our brain's best guess to provide information that will motivate us in a particular way. As such, emotions are somewhat like a person in your life who gives you information that is vital to your goals, but at other times what he or she offers is misguided as a result of his or her own past experiences. Accept the information, silently consider and explore possibilities, and arrive at a conclusion.

Both children and the adults in their lives can benefit from understanding the source of what motivates them. Mistakenly, many parents, teachers, and even some psychological researchers believe only positive emotions motivate children in a healthy way, yet how many children have a motivational system that will trigger the emotion of excitement, for example, in response to several pages of math problems or taking out the garbage? Although children can be motivated by anticipating that they will feel positive emotions that result in pride, often what motivates a child to get something done has to do with his or her response to negative emotions, such as the avoidance of shame or guilt or a relief from distress. In any case, the ultimate goals to keep in mind have to do with consistently meeting deadlines and using one's best efforts, but the way in which these goals are accomplished may vary.

Even so, many parents attempt to motivate children or offset a negative emotional response to a task they must complete by offering a later reward. Another tactic involves a punitive response, such as taking away a privilege or an activity until a task has been completed. Some children, however, may prefer to avoid the negative emotion associated with getting something done rather than endure what they have to do to gain a future reward or avoid punishment. Unfortunately, at the extreme, some adults behave in ways that activate fear, shame, or distress responses in children to stimulate their getting something done. In such situations the adult misuses the child's emotional system for his or her own goals, that is, controlling the child's behavior through activating negative emotion. People who bully operate on a similar principle. Instead, educators or caregivers who can be playful with their awareness of how the human motivational system works can activate interest or excitement about the relief that will be felt in completing a dreaded task, along with pride in the outcome. That's real.

Sadly, children are not redirected when they translate in misguided or maladaptive ways what their motivational system is informing them to do. Just because we experience a negative emotion about a task to complete does not mean we should avoid getting something done or be punished for what is felt. Moreover, many children are confused when they do not feel any positive emotion about a task that is before them, as though that's always how they should feel.

It's important at any age to learn about yourself by taking a look at your reactions to the emotions you feel. As discussed in several chapters of this book, self-observation that is often prompted by shame and felt as regret provides an opportunity to learn, change, improve, or do something differently the next time around. Both deadline-driven procrastinators and task-driven nonprocrastinators who are successful in their endeavors or careers often make use of the emotions they experience. Rather than defensively respond to what they feel, they instead reflect, self-evaluate, and learn.

Evolution has given you an impressive motivational system to help you navigate through life and get things done. Just like the thumb on your hand, emotions have evolved to help you, even though, at times, they may seem to get in the way. You may think that the best course of action is to suppress or disregard an intense emotion rather than figure it out, but why ignore an emotion that has evolved over thousands of years to help you? Emotions serve a purpose, informing you, the operator of your body, what to do. If you learn to interpret the messages your emotions convey and understand your reactions to them, you can make the most of the system that not only motivates you to get things done but also motivates everything you do.

NOTES

INTRODUCTION

1. Silvan S. Tomkins, *Affect Imagery Consciousness* (New York: Springer, 2008), 68. The affect theorist Silvan Tomkins explains that we have evolved with an affect (emotional) system whereby some affects feel good and some feel bad. Thus, humans are motivated to maximize positive affect or to reduce negative affect.

2. Piers Steel, "The Nature of Procrastination: A Meta-Analytic and Theoretical Review of Quintessential Self-Regulatory Failure," *Psychological Bulletin* 133 (2007): 65–94. Steel's paper provides a comprehensive review of many procrastination studies.

3. Lisa Zarick and Robert Stonebracker, "I'll Do It Tomorrow: The Logic of Procrastination," *College Teaching* 57 (2009): 211–15.

4. Steel, "The Nature of Procrastination," 65.

5. Michael Wohl, Timothy Pychyl, and Shannon Bennett, "I Forgive Myself, Now I Can Study: How Self-Forgiveness for Procrastinating Can Reduce Future Procrastination," *Personality and Individual Differences* 48 (2010): 803–808.

CHAPTER I. WHAT MOTIVATES GETTING THINGS DONE

1. *Merriam-Webster Dictionary, s.v.* "Procrastinate," accessed October 27, 2015, http://www.merriam-webster.com/dictionary/procrastinate.

CHAPTER 2. DEADLINES, DELIBERATION, AND DISTRACTION

1. In survey and interview data I collected from over 400 successful professionals—including business executives, attorneys, health professionals, entrepreneurs, academics, and visionaries—task-driven people indicated their tendency to get things done as soon as possible and did not miss deadlines. However, deadline-driven individuals, as well, revealed they rarely, if ever, miss deadlines, including those who self-identified as extreme procrastinators.

2. Most participants in my survey self-identified as either a procrastinator (43 percent) or not (40 percent); 17 percent chose the middle ground of the five-point scale. However, the majority of this group, as indicated by their choices on other survey items, was far more inclined to procrastinate.

3. Angela Hsin Chen Chu and Jin Nam Choi, "Rethinking Procrastination: Positive Effects of 'Active' Procrastination Behavior on Attitudes and Performance," *Journal of Social Psychology* 145, no. 3 (2005): 245–64.

4. Timothy A. Pychyl, Richard W. Morin, and Brian R. Salmon, "Procrastination and the Planning Fallacy: An Examination of the Study Habits of University Students," *Journal of Social Behavior and Personality* 15, no. 5 (2000): 135.

5. Joachim Stoeber, Rachel A. Harris, and Paul S. Moon, "Perfectionism and the Experience of Pride, Shame, and Guilt: Comparing Healthy Perfectionists, Unhealthy Perfectionists, and Nonperfectionists," *Personality and Individual Differences* 43, no. 1 (2007): 131–41.

6. My survey data significantly indicated that both procrastinators and nonprocrastinators were "bothered" by uncompleted tasks. However, the more people identified as procrastinators, the less they felt compelled to rid themselves of the thought that a task remained incomplete. However, at a significant level, task-driven people indicated a desire to complete tasks early to free themselves from thinking about something that remained unfinished.

7. Joseph Ferrari and Timothy Pychyl, "'If I Wait My Partner Will Do It': The Role of Conscientiousness as a Mediator in the Relation of Academic Procrastination and Perceived Social Loafing," *North American Journal of Psychology* 14 (2012): 13–24.

8. David A. Rosenbaum, Lanyun Gong, and Cory Adam Potts, "Pre-Crastination: Hastening Subgoal Completion at the Expense of Extra Physical Effort," *Psychological Science* 25, no. 7 (2014): 1487.

9. Eliaz Segal, "Incubation in Insight Problem Solving," *Creativity Research Journal* 16, no. 1 (2004): 141–48.

10. Ibid., 144.

11. Jennifer Wiley and Andrew F. Jarosz, "Working Memory Capacity, Attentional Focus, and Problem Solving," *Current Directions in Psychological Sciences* 21, no. 4 (2012): 258.

12. My survey data indicated that task-driven and deadline-driven people did not differ significantly in the degree to which they worried or thought about tasks that were not completed.

13. Piers Steel, "The Nature of Procrastination: A Meta-Analytic and Theoretical Review of Quintessential Self-Regulatory Failure," *Psychological Bulletin* 133 (2007): 81–84. Heretofore, researchers have primarily attributed psychopathology to procrastinators who are distracted or inactive prior to a task deadline. One such example is Steel's "temporal motivation theory" in which procrastination behavior is explained in terms of the inclination of procrastinators to pursue goals that are pleasurable and have large and immediate rewards while putting off tasks that are unpleasant, have lackluster qualities, or offer compensation in the distant future.

14. Joseph R. Ferrari, Judith L. Johnson, and William G. McCown, *Procrastination and Task Avoidance: Theory, Research, and Treatment* (New York: Springer, 1995/2013), 110. Some procrastination researchers speculate that the delay of task completion relieves feelings of anxiety related to the avoidance of difficult or boring tasks, as well as provides relief from confirming one's fears concerning a lack of ability; yet such speculation has not been verified.

15. Jennifer Lavoie and Timothy Pychyl, "Cyberslacking and the Procrastination Superhighway: A Web-Based Survey of Online Procrastination, Attitudes, and Emotion," *Social Science Computer Review* 19, no. 4 (2001): 431–44.

16. Pychyl et al., "Procrastination and the Planning Fallacy," 135.

CHAPTER 3. WHAT MOTIVATES EARLY ACTION OR DELAY?

1. Silvan S. Tomkins, *Affect Imagery Consciousness* (New York: Springer, 2008), 68.

2. Ibid., xi–xx. The words "emotion" and "affect" are often used interchangeably. Affects are the unconscious and biological source of primary motivating mechanisms, which are experienced consciously as feelings and through memory become emotions. While I use the term "emotion" throughout this chapter, I make a distinction between the biology of emotion, technically called affect, and emotion per se, which is our common experience of feeling embedded in our history with those feelings. This is our emotional biography. The affect is biologically universal and contains no verbal meanings, whereas

our experience of emotion involves language and past experience. But since our common experience is emotion, I use that term in this chapter.

3. Paul Ekman, "Facial Expression and Emotion," *American Psychologist* 48, no. 4 (1993): 384–92.

4. Ibid., 387.

5. Paul Ekman, "Basic Emotions," in *Handbook of Cognition and Emotion*, ed. Tim Dalgleish and Mick Power (Sussex: John Wiley & Sons, 1999), 55.

6. Tara L. Gruenwald, Sally S. Dickerson, and Margaret E. Kemeny, "A Social Function for Self-Conscious Emotions: The Social Self-Preservation Theory," in *The Self-Conscious Emotions: Theory and Research*, ed. Jessica L. Tracy, Richard W. Robins, and June Price Tangney (New York: Guilford, 2007), 72–74.

7. Rebecca M. Todd, William A. Cunningham, Adam K. Anderson, and Evan Thompson, "Affect-Biased Attention as Emotion Regulation," *Trends in Cognitive Science* 16, no. 7 (2012), 365, http://dx.doi.org/10.1016/j.tics.2012.06.003.

8. Arne Öhman, Anders Flykt, and Francisco Esteves, "Emotion Drives Attention: Detecting the Snake in the Grass," *Journal of Experimental Psychology, General* 130, no. 3 (2001), 467, doi: 10.1037/AXJ96-3445.130.3.466.

9. Silvan S. Tomkins, "Script Theory," in *Exploring Affect: The Selected Writings of Silvan S. Tomkins*, ed. E. Virginia Demos (New York: Cambridge University Press, 1995), 334.

10. Ibid., 387.

11. Ibid., 290.

12. Ibid.

13. Donald Nathanson, *Shame and Pride: Affects, Sex, and the Birth of the Self* (New York: Norton, 1992), 311.

14. Silvan S. Tomkins, "The Quest for Primary Motives: Biography and Autobiography of an Idea," in *Exploring Affect: The Selected Writings of Silvan S. Tomkins*, ed. E. Virginia Demos (New York: Cambridge University Press, 1995), 59.

15. Iain McGilchrist, *The Master and His Emissary: The Divided Brain and the Making of the Western World* (New Haven: Yale University Press, 2009), 184.

16. Lisa Zarick and Robert Stonebraker, "I'll Do It Tomorrow: The Logic of Procrastination," *College Teaching* 57, no. 4 (2009), 214.

17. Richard S. Lazarus, "Cognition and Motivation in Emotion," *American Psychologist* 46, no. 4 (1991), 354.

18. Ibid.

19. Dacher Keltner and Jennifer Lerner, "Emotion," in *Handbook of Social Psychology*, 5th ed., ed. Susan T. Fiske, Daniel T. Gilbert, and Gardner Lindsey (New York: McGraw-Hill, 2010), 315.

20. Barbara Fredrickson, "The Role of Positive Emotions in Positive Psychology: The Broaden-and-Build Theory of Positive Emotions," *American Psychologist* 56, no. 3 (2001), 218, doi: 10.1037//0003-066X.56.3.218.

21. Carol Sansone, Charlene Weir, Lora Harpster, and Carolyn Morgan, "Once a Boring Task Always a Boring Task? Interest as a Self-Regulatory Mechanism," *Journal of Personality and Social Psychology* 63, no. 3 (1992), 379.

CHAPTER 4. ANXIETY AS AN ENGINE OF TASK COMPLETION

1. Carroll E. Izard, *Human Emotions* (New York: Plenum, 1977), 93.

2. *Merriam-Webster Dictionary, s.v.* "Anxiety," accessed March 17, 2016, http://www.merriam-webster.com/dictionary/anxiety. The *Merriam-Webster Dictionary* defines anxiety as "1) painful or apprehensive uneasiness of mind usually over an impending or anticipated ill; fearful concern or interest; a cause of anxiety. 2) an abnormal and overwhelming sense of apprehension and fear often marked by physiological signs (such as sweating, tension, and increased pulse), by doubt concerning the reality and nature of the threat, and by self-doubt about one's capacity to cope with it."

3. Donald Nathanson, *Shame and Pride: Affect, Sex, and the Birth of the Self* (New York: Norton, 1992), 59. "Affect is the engine that drives us," asserted Nathanson.

4. Phan Luu, Don M. Tucker, and Douglas Derryberry, "Anxiety and the Motivational Basis of Working Memory," *Cognitive Therapy and Research* 22, no. 6 (1998): 577.

5. Silvan S. Tomkins, *Affect Imagery Consciousness* (New York: Springer, 1962/2008), 584.

6. Sigmund Freud, "Introductory Lectures on Psychoanalysis. Part III. General Theory of the Neurosis, Lecture XXV: Anxiety (1916)," in *Standard Edition of the Complete Psychological Works of Sigmund Freud*, trans. James Strachey (London: Hogarth Press, 1978), 392.

7. Sigmund Freud, "New Introductory Lectures on Psychoanalysis. Lecture XXII: Anxiety and Instinctual Life (1933)," in *Standard Edition of the Complete Psychological Works of Sigmund Freud*, trans. James Strachey (London: Hogarth Press, 1978), 81–111.

8. Nathanson, *Shame and Pride*, 95.

9. American Psychiatric Association, *Diagnostic and Statistical Manual of Mental Disorders*, 5th ed. (Washington, DC: American Psychiatric Publishing, 2013), 189–234.

10. Carroll Izard et al., "Self-Organization of Discrete Emotions, Emotion Patterns, and Emotion-Cognition Relations," in *Emotion, Development, and Self-Organization: Dynamic Systems Approaches to Emotional Development* (Cambridge Studies in Social and Emotional Development), ed. by Marc D. Lewis and Isabela Granic (New York: Cambridge University Press, 2000), 19; Arne Öhman, "Fear and Anxiety: Overlaps and Dissociations," in *Handbook of Emotions*, ed. Marc D. Lewis, Jeannette M. Haviland-Jones, and Lisa Feldman Barrett (New York: The Guilford Press, 2010), 709–29.

11. Peter J. Lang, Michael Davis, and Arne Öhman, "Fear and Anxiety: Animal Models and Human Cognitive Psychophysiology," *Journal of Affective Disorders* 61, no. 3 (2000): 137–59, doi: 10.1016/S0165-0327(00)00343-8.

12. Patrick Sylvers, Scott O. Lilienfeld, and Jamie L. LaPrairie, "Differences Between Trait Fear and Trait Anxiety: Implications for Psychopathology," *Clinical Psychology Review* 31, no. 1 (2011): 122, doi: 10.1016/j.cpr.2010.08.004.

13. Lang et al., "Fear and Anxiety," 137.

14. Izard, *Human Emotions*, 93.

15. Ibid., 378.

16. Ibid.

17. Silvan S. Tomkins, "The Quest for Primary Motives: Biography and Autobiography of an Idea," in *Exploring Affect: The Selected Writings of Silvan S. Tomkins*, ed. E. Virginia Demos (New York: Cambridge University Press, 1995), 47.

18. Nathanson, *Shame and Pride*, 99.

19. Abiola Keller et al., "Does the Perception That Stress Affects Health Matter? The Association with Health and Mortality," *Health Psychology* 31, no. 5 (2012): 677, doi: 10.1037/a0026743.

20. According to my survey data, professionally successful people, regardless of their task-completion style, on average appear to worry similarly about uncompleted tasks, but the action they are compelled to take based on that worry differs considerably. In the narratives I collected, worry, as a cognitive magnification of distress or fear, created stress immediately for task-driven participants and laid in the back of the minds of deadline-driven participants until they were motivated by a deadline.

21. William G. Sommer, "Procrastination and Cramming: How Adept Students Ace the System," *Journal of American College Health* 39, no. 1 (1990): 6, doi: 10.1080/07448481.1990.9936207.

22. Tomkins, "The Quest for Primary Motives, 57–58.

23. David Barlow, "Disorders of Emotion," *Psychological Inquiry* 2, no. 1 (1991): 58–71.

24. Carroll Izard, "Affect, Awareness, and Performance," in *Affect, Cognition, and Personality*, eds. Silvan Tomkins and Carroll Izard (London: Tavistock Publications, 1965), 22.

25. Luu et al., "Anxiety and the Motivational Basis of Working Memory," 577. Emphasizing that anxiety must be appreciated as a general motivational control, the authors note that anxiety is not simply a distraction to thinking but that it may fundamentally and adaptively motivate cognition. They maintain that the attention-focusing quality of anxiety may play a prominent role in left hemisphere analytic cognition.

26. Donald A. Norman, "Emotion and Design: Attractive Things Work Better," *Interactions Magazine* 9 (2002): 36.

27. Douglas Derryberry and Marjorie Reed, "Anxiety and Attentional Focusing: Trait, State and Hemispheric Influences," *Personality and Individual Differences* 25, no. 4 (1998): 745; Sadia Najmi, Jennie M. Kuckertz, and Nader Amir, "Attentional Impairment in Anxiety: Inefficiency in Expanding the Scope of Attention," *Depression and Anxiety* 29, no. 3 (2012): 243, doi: 10.1002/da.20900.

28. See, for example, Joseph R. Ferrari and Juan Francisco Diaz-Morales, "Procrastination: Different Time Orientations Reflect Different Motives," *Journal of Research in Personality* 41, no. 3 (2007): 712, doi: 10.1016/j.jrp.2006.06.006; William McCown, Thomas Petzel, and Patricia Rupert, "An Experimental Study of Some Hypothesized Behaviors and Personality Variables of College Student Procrastinators," *Personality and Individual Differences* 8, no. 6 (1987): 781–86; Clarry H. Lay et al., "An Assessment of Appraisal, Anxiety, Coping, and Procrastination During an Examination Period," *European Journal of Personality* 3, no. 3 (1989): 195–208, doi: 10.1002/per.2410030305; Gregory Schraw, Theresa Wadkins, and Lori Olafson, "Doing the Things We Do: A Grounded Theory of Academic Procrastination," *Journal of Educational Psychology* 99, no. 1 (2007): 12–25.

29. Esther D. Rothblum, Laura J. Solomon, and Janice Murakami, "Affective, Cognitive, and Behavioral Differences Between High and Low Procrastinators," *Journal of Counseling Psychology* 33, no. 4 (1986): 387–88.

30. Allison Wood Brooks, "Get Excited: Reappraising Pre-Performance Anxiety as Excitement," *Journal of Experimental Psychology, General* 143, no. 3 (2014): 1153–54.

31. Ibid., 1144.

32. Jeremy Jamieson, Wendy Berry Mendes, and Matthew K. Nock, "Improving Acute Stress Responses: The Power of Reappraisal," *Current Direc-*

tions of Psychological Science 22, no. 1 (2013): 51, doi: 10.1177/0963721412461500.

33. Robert M. Yerkes and John D. Dodson, "The Relationship of Stimulus to Rapidity of Habit Formation," *Journal of Comparative Neurology and Psychology* 18, no. 5 (1908): 459. In their investigation of anxiety Yerkes and Dodson also predicted there are optimal levels of arousal in learning tasks—an inverted U-shaped function between arousal and performance—which became known as the *Yerkes-Dodson law*.

34. Clarence Leuba, "Toward Some Integration of Learning Theories: The Concept of Optimal Stimulation," *Psychological Report* 1 (1955): 27, doi: 10.2466/PR0.1.27-33.

35. Daniel Gould and Suzanne Tuffey, "Zones of Optimal Functioning Research: A Review and Critique," *Anxiety, Stress, and Coping* 9, no. 1 (1996): 53–68, doi: 10.1080/10615809608249392.

36. Mihaly Csikszentmihalyi, *Flow: The Psychology of Optimal Experience* (New York: Harper Perennial, 1990), 5–7.

37. Schraw et al., "Doing the Things We Do," 11–13.

38. Jane B. Burka and Lenora M. Yuen, *Procrastination: Why You Do It and What to Do About It Now* (Boston: DaCapo Lifelong Books, 2008), 54; Joseph Ferrari, Kelly Barnes, and Piers Steel, "Life Regrets by Avoidant Procrastinators: Why Put Off Today What You Will Regret Tomorrow?" *Journal of Individual Differences* 30, no. 3 (2009): 163–64, doi: 0.1027/1614-0001.30.3.163.

39. W. Kyle Simpson and Timothy A. Pychyl, "In Search of the Arousal Procrastinator: Investigating the Relation between Procrastination, Arousal-Based Personality Traits and Beliefs about Motivations," *Personality and Individual Differences* 47, no. 8 (2009), 906, doi: 10.1016/j.paid.2009.07.013.

40. Ibid., 910.

41. Schraw et al., "Doing the Things We Do," 11–13.

42. Lay et al., "An Assessment of Appraisal Anxiety," 204–206.

43. James Awuni Azure, "Correlates of Anxiety and Academic Procrastination in Higher Education," *Global Journal of Educational Research* 10, no. 1 (2011): 61–62.

44. Leon Wurmser, "Shame: The Veiled Companion of Narcissism," in *The Many Faces of Shame*, ed. Donald Nathanson (New York: Guilford Press, 1987), 68.

CHAPTER 5. WHY YOU SHOULD FEAR FAILURE

1. Esther D. Rothblum, Laura J. Solomon, and Janice Murakami, "Affective, Cognitive, and Behavioral Differences Between High and Low Procrastinators," *Journal of Counseling Psychology* 33, no. 4 (1986): 388; Jane B. Burka and Lenora M. Yuen, *Procrastination: Why You Do It and What to Do About It Now* (Boston: DaCapo Lifelong Books, 2008), 19–32.

2. Henri C. Schouwenburg, "Procrastinators and Fear of Failure: An Exploration of Reasons for Procrastination," *European Journal of Personality* 6, no. 3 (1992): 225, doi: 10.1002/per.2410060305.

3. Ibid.

4. In my survey data participants indicated to a highly significant degree that a "fear of failure" gives them energy for task completion.

5. Holly A. McGregor and Andrew J. Elliot, "The Shame of Failure: Examining the Link Between Fear of Failure and Shame," *Personality and Social Psychology Bulletin* 3, no. 2 (2005): 218, doi: 10.1177/0146167204271420.

6. Leon Wurmser, "Shame: The Veiled Companion of Narcissism," in *The Many Faces of Shame*, ed. Donald Nathanson (New York: Guilford Press, 1987), 68.

7. Gregory Schraw, Theresa Wadkins, and Lori Olafson, "Doing the Things We Do: A Grounded Theory of Academic Procrastination," *Journal of Educational Psychology* 99, no. 1 (2007): 23, doi: 10.1037/0022–0663.99.1.12.

8. Donald Nathanson, *Shame and Pride: Affect, Sex, and the Birth of the Self* (New York: Norton, 1992), 87.

9. Ibid., 356.

10. June Tangney, Rowland S. Miller, Laura Flicker, and Deborah Hill Barlow, "Are Shame, Guilt, and Embarrassment Distinct Emotions?" *Journal of Personality and Social Psychology* 70 (1996): 1256–59.

11. Nathanson, *Shame and Pride*, 317.

12. Ibid., 138–40; Silvan S. Tomkins, *Affect Imagery Consciousness* (New York: Springer, 2008), 360–61.

13. Michael Franz Basch, "The Concept of Affect: A Re-Examination," *Journal of the American Psychoanalytic Association* 24 (1976): 763; Allan A. Schore, *Affect Regulation and the Repair of the Self* (New York: Norton, 2003), 158; Colwyn Trevarthen and Kenneth Aiken, "Infant Intersubjectivity: Research, Theory, and Clinical Applications," *Journal of Child Psychology and Psychiatry* 42, no. 1 (2001): 5.

14. Basch, "The Concept of Affect," 763; Schore, *Affect Regulation*, 158; Trevarthen and Aiken, "Infant Intersubjectivity," 5.

15. Basch, "The Concept of Affect," 763; Schore, *Affect Regulation*, 158.

16. Basch, "The Concept of Affect," 763; Schore, *Affect Regulation*, 171.

17. Nathanson, *Shame and Pride*, 316.

18. Paul Gilbert, "Evolution, Attractiveness, and the Emergence of Shame and Guilt in a Self-Aware Mind: A Reflection on Tracy and Robins," *Psychological Inquiry* 15, no. 2 (2004): 15.

19. Tomkins, *Affect Imagery Consciousness*, 366.

20. Jennifer S. Beer and Dacher Keltner, "What Is Unique About the Self-Conscious Emotions?" *Psychological Inquiry* 15, no. 2 (2004): 127.

21. Nathanson, *Shame and Pride*, 19.

22. Michael Lewis, "Self-Conscious Emotions: Embarrassment, Pride, Shame, and Guilt," in *Handbook of Emotions*, 3rd ed., ed. Michael Lewis, Jeannette M. Haviland-Jones, and Lisa Feldman Barrett (New York: Guilford Press, 2008), 749–50.

23. Tomkins, *Affect, Imagery, Counsciousness*, 368.

24. Nathanson, *Shame and Pride*, 327.

25. See Nathalie Camille et al., "The Involvement of the Orbitofrontal Cortex in the Experience of Regret," *Science* 304, no. 5674 (2004): 1167, doi: 10.1126/science.1094550. Researchers found that people with orbitofrontal cortical lesions do not anticipate negative consequences of their choices and do not report regret and normal subjects chose to minimize future regret and learned from their emotional experience involved with their counterfactual thinking.

26. Marcel Zeelenberg et al., "Emotional Reactions to the Outcomes of Decisions: The Role of Counterfactual Thought in the Experience of Regret and Disappointment," *Organizational Behavior and Human Decision Processes* 75, no. 2 (1998): 117, doi: 10.1006/obhd.1998.2784.

27. Joseph Ferrari, Kelly Barnes, and Piers Steel, "Life Regrets by Avoidant Procrastinators: Why Put Off Today What You Will Regret Tomorrow?" *Journal of Individual Differences* 30, no. 3 (2009): 163.

28. Nathanson, *Shame and Pride*, 211.

29. Andrew Martin, Herbert Marsh, and Raymond Debus, "A Quadripolar Need Achievement Representation of Self-Handicapping and Defensive Pessimism," *American Educational Research Journal* 38, no. 3 (2001): 583.

30. Gilbert, "Evolution, Attractiveness, and the Emergence of Shame and Guilt," 133.

31. Andrew J. Elliot and Marcy A. Church, "A Hierarchical Model of Approach and Avoidance Achievement Motivation," *Journal of Personality and Social Psychology* 72, no. 1 (1997): 229.

32. Jeannine E. Turner and Diane L. Schallert, "Expectancy-Value Relationships of Shame Reactions and Shame Resiliency," *Journal of Educational Psychology* 93, no. 2 (2001): 320.

33. Nathanson, *Shame and Pride*, 305–14.

34. Ibid., 315–25.

35. Ibid.

36. Ibid., 336–59.

37. Ibid., 360–77.

38. Ibid.

39. Christopher A. Wolters, "Understanding Procrastination from a Self-Regulated Learning Perspective," *Journal of Educational Psychology* 95, no. 1 (2003): 179–87.

40. Dianne M. Tice, Ellen Bratslavsky, and Roy F. Baumeister, "Emotional Distress Regulation Takes Precedence Over Impulse Control: If You Feel Bad, Do It!" *Journal of Personality and Social Psychology* 80, no. 1 (2001): 53–67, doi: 10.1037//0022-3514.80.1.53.

41. Bill McCown, Thomas Petzel, and Patricia Rupert, "An Experimental Study of Some Hypothesized Behaviors and Personality Variables of College Student Procrastinators," *Personality and Individual Differences* 8, no. 6 (1987): 781–86; Henri C. Schouwenburg and Clarry H. Lay, "Trait Procrastination and the Big-Five Factors of Personality," *Personality and Individual Differences* 18, no. 4 (1995): 481–90.

42. Allan K. Blunt and Timothy A. Pychyl, "Task Aversiveness and Procrastination: A Multi-Dimensional Approach to Task Aversiveness Across Stages of Personal Projects," *Personality and Individual Differences* 28, no. 1 (2000): 153–67; Noach Milgram, Sergio Marshevsky, and Chaya Sadeh, "Correlates of Academic Procrastination: Discomfort, Task Aversiveness, and Task Capability," *Journal of Psychology: Interdisciplinary and Applied* 129, no. 2 (1995): 145–55.

43. Joseph R. Ferrari, "Procrastination in the Workplace: Attributions for Failure Among Individuals with Similar Behavioral Tendencies," *Journal of Individual Differences* 13, no. 3 (1992), 315–19, doi: 10.1016/0191-8869(92)90108-2.

44. Joseph R. Ferrari and Brett L. Beck, "Affective Responses Before and After Fraudulent Excuses by Academic Procrastinators," *Education* 118, no. 4 (1998), 529–37; Miguel Roig and Lauren DeTommaso, "Are College Cheating and Plagiarism Related to Academic Procrastination?" *Psychological Reports* 77 (1995): 691–98.

45. Brett L. Beck, Susan R. Koons, and Debra L. Milgrim, "Correlates and Consequences of Behavioral Procrastination: The Effects of Academic Procrastination, Self-Consciousness, Self-Esteem and Self-Handicapping," *Journal of Social Behavior and Personality* 15, no. 5 (2000): 3–13; Joseph R. Ferrari and Dianne M. Tice, "Procrastination as a Self-Handicap for Men and Women: A Task-Avoidance Strategy in a Laboratory Setting," *Journal of Research in*

Personality 34, no. 1 (2000): 73–83. doi: http://dx.doi.org/10.1006/jrpe.1999.2261.

46. Caroline Senecal, Etienne Julien, and Frederic Guay, "Role Conflict and Academic Procrastination: A Self-Determination Perspective," *European Journal of Social Psychology* 33, (2003): 135–45. doi: 10.1002/ejsp.144.

47. Rhonda L. Fee and June P. Tangney, "Procrastination: A Means of Avoiding Shame or Guilt?" *Journal of Social Behavior and Personality* 15, no. 5 (2000): 167–84.

48. Schouwenburg, "Procrastinators and Fear of Failure," 225–36.

49. Nathanson, *Shame and Pride*, 460.

CHAPTER 6. PURSUING EXCELLENCE

1. Ninety-five percent of my survey respondents who had answered very affirmatively to the statement that others would consider them professionally successful also responded very affirmatively to the statement "I'm somewhat of a 'perfectionist'—I tend to want to do things very well." Identifying with being a "somewhat of a perfectionist" was also highly correlated with having a motivating "fear of failure."

2. Christine Quinn Trank, Sara L. Rynes, and Robert D. Bretz Jr., "Attracting Applicants in the War for Talent: Differences in Work Preferences Among High Achievers," *Journal of Business and Psychology* 16, no. 3 (2002): 331–45.

3. Mustafa Sarkar and David Fletcher, "Ordinary Magic, Extraordinary Performance: Psychological Resilience and Thriving in High Achievers," *Sport, Exercise, and Performance Psychology* 3, no. 1 (2014): 56, doi: 0.1037/spy0000003; Mary J. Dickinson and David A. G. Dickinson, "Practically Perfect in Every Way: Can Reframing Perfectionism for High-Achieving Undergraduates Impact Academic Resilience?" *Studies in Higher Education* 40, no. 10 (2015): 1889.

4. Ibid., 351.

5. Ibid., 341.

6. Ibid.

7. Alice Lo and Maree J. Abbott, "Review of the Theoretical, Empirical, and Clinical Status of Adaptive and Maladaptive Perfectionism," *Behaviour Change* 30, no. 2 (2013): 96–116. For an excellent review of the theoretical, empirical, and clinical status of perfectionism, see this review.

8. Peter J. Bieling, Anne L. Israeli, and Martin M. Antony, "Is Perfectionism Good, Bad, or Both? Examining Models of the Perfectionism Construct," *Personality and Individual Differences* 36, no. 6 (2004): 1373; KoUn Eum and

Kenneth G. Rice, "Test Anxiety, Perfectionism, Goal Orientation, and Academic Performance," *Anxiety, Stress & Coping: An International Journal* 24, no. 2 (2011), 175; Don E. Hamachek, "Psychodynamics of Normal and Neurotic Perfectionism," *Psychology* 15, no. 1 (1978), 27.

9. Sarkar and Fletcher, "Ordinary Magic, Extraordinary Performance," 56.

10. Jeff Szymanski, *The Perfectionist's Handbook: Take Risks, Invite Criticism, and Make the Most of Your Mistakes* (New York: Wiley, 2011), 3–12.

11. Hamachek, "Psychodynamics of Normal and Neurotic Perfectionism," 27.

12. Szymanski, *The Perfectionist's Handbook*, 3–12.

13. Paul L. Hewitt and Gordon L. Flett, "Perfectionism in Self and Social Contexts: Conceptualization, Assessment, and Association with Psychopathology," *Journal of Personality and Social Psychology* 60, no. 3 (1991): 457–58.

14. Gordon L. Flett et al., "Perfectionism, Self-Actualization, and Personal Adjustment," *Journal of Social Behavior and Personality* 6, no. 5 (1991): 147.

15. David E. Conroy, Miranda P. Kaye, and Angela M. Fifer, "Cognitive Links Between Fear of Failure and Perfectionism," *Journal of Rational-Emotive & Cognitive-Behavior Therapy* 25, no. 4 (2007): 237.

16. Anthony J. Onwuegbuzie, "Academic Procrastinators and Perfectionistic Tendencies among Graduate Students," *Journal of Social Behavior & Personality* 15, no. 5 (2000), 103.

17. Ibid., 103–109; Douglas Saddler and Laurie A. Sacks, "Multidimensional Perfectionism and Academic Procrastination: Relationships with Depression in University Students," *Psychological Reports* 73, no. 3 (1994), 103.

18. Kenneth G. Rice, Clarissa M. E. Richardson, and Dustin Clark, "Perfectionism, Procrastination, and Psychological Distress," *Journal of Counseling Psychology* 59, no. 2. (2012): 299, doi: 0.1037/a0026643.

19. Ronda L. Fee and June P. Tangney, "Procrastination: A Means of Avoiding Shame or Guilt?" *Journal of Social Behavior and Personality* 50, no. 5 (2000): 182.

20. Robert R. McCrae and Paul T. Costa, Jr., "The Five Factor Theory of Personality," in *Handbook of Personality: Theory and Research*, ed. Oliver P. John, Richard W. Robins, and Lawrence A. Pervin (New York: Guilford Press, 2008), 159–81; Lewis R. Goldberg, "The Structure of Phenotypic Personality Traits," *American Psychologist* 48, no. 1 (1993), 26–34.

21. Paul T. Costa Jr. and Robert R. McCrae, "Domains and Facets: Hierarchical Personality Assessment Using the Revised NEO Personality Inventory," *Journal of Personality Assessment* 64, no. 1 (1995), 28.

22. Joachim Stoeber, Kathleen Otto, and Claudia Dalbert, "Perfectionism and the Big Five: Conscientiousness Predicts Longitudinal Increases in Self-

Oriented Perfectionism," *Personality and Individual Differences* 47, no. 4 (2009), 363.

23. Onwuegbuzie, "Academic Procrastinators and Perfectionistic Tendencies," 863.

24. Oliver P. John, "The Big Five Personality Project Test," *OutOfService*, July 3, 2016, http://www.outofservice.com/bigfive/.

25. Joachim Stoeber, Tom Kempe, and Ellen J. Keogh, "Facets of Self-Oriented and Socially Prescribed Perfectionism and Feelings of Pride, Shame, and Guilt Following Success and Failure," *Personality and Individual Differences* 44, no. 7 (2008), 1513, doi: 10.1016/j.paid.2008.01.007.

26. Randy Frost and Patricia A. Marten, "Perfectionism and Evaluative Threat," *Cognitive Therapy and Research* 14, no. 6 (1990), 559.

CHAPTER 7. RELATIONSHIPS AND DIVERGENT MOTIVATIONAL STYLES

1. J. Samuel Bois, *Communication as Creative Experience* (Los Angeles: Viewpoints Institute, 1968), 24.

2. Jeffrey Pfeffer and Robert I. Sutton, "Evidenced-Based Management," *Harvard Business Review* 84, no. 1 (2006): 65. As Pfeffer and Sutton note: "In Western culture, people believe that the early bird gets the worm, yet this is a half-truth. As futurist Paul Saffo puts it, the whole truth is that the second (or third or fourth) mouse often gets the cheese. Unfortunately, beliefs in the power of being first and fastest in everything we do are so ingrained that giving people contradictory evidence does not cause them to abandon their faith in the first-mover advantage. Beliefs rooted in ideology or in cultural values are quite 'sticky,' resist disconfirmation, and persist in affecting judgments and choice, regardless of whether they are true."

3. Joseph R. Ferrari, "Procrastination in the Workplace: Attributions for Failure Among Individuals with Similar Behavioral Tendencies," *Personality and Individual Differences* 13, no. 3 (1992): 315, doi: 10.1016/0191-8869(92)90108-2.

4. Ibid., 318.

5. Brian K. Payne and Elizabeth Monk-Turner, "Students' Perceptions of Group Projects: The Role of Race, Age, and Slacking," *College Student Journal* 40, no. 1 (2006): 132.

6. Ibid., 138–39.

7. Scott A. Myers et al., "Dealing with Slackers in College Classroom Work Groups," *College Student Journal* 43, no. 2 (2009): 596.

8. Ibid., 597.

9. Clarry H. Lay, "Trait Procrastination, Agitation, Dejection, and Self-Discrepancy," in *Procrastination and Task Avoidance: Theory, Research, and Treatment*, ed. Joseph Ferrari, Judith Johnson, and William G. McCown (New York: Plenum, 1995), 97–100.

10. Gordon L. Flett, Kirk R. Blankstein, and Thomas R. Martin, "Procrastination, Negative Self-Evaluation, and Stress in Depression and Anxiety," in *Procrastination and Task Avoidance: Theory, Research, and Treatment*, ed. Joseph Ferrari, Judith Johnson, and William G. McCown (New York: Plenum, 1995), 138–48.

11. Donald L. Nathanson, *Shame and Pride: Affect, Sex, and the Birth of the Self* (New York: Norton, 1992), 69.

12. Ibid., 62.

13. Ibid., 132–37.

14. Ibid., 145.

15. Ibid., 303–77.

16. Ibid., 95.

17. Ibid., 211.

CHAPTER 8. OPTIMIZING YOUR MOTIVATIONAL STYLE

1. David Wolman, *A Left Hand Turn Around the World: Chasing the Mystery and Meaning of All Things Southpaw* (Boston: DaCapo Press, 2006), 15.

2. Alison Wood Brooks, "Get Excited: Reappraising Pre-Performance Anxiety as Excitement," *Journal of Experimental Psychology, General* 3, no. 143 (2013): 1144.

3. Ibid., 1146.

4. Ibid., 1154.

5. Ibid., 1155.

6. Jeremy P. Jamieson, Matthew K. Nock, and Wendy Berry Mendes, "Mind Over Matter: Reappraising Arousal Improves Cardiovascular and Cognitive Responses to Stress," *Journal of Experimental Psychology, General* 141, no. 3 (2012): 417, doi: http://dx.doi.org/10.1037/a0025719.

7. Jeremy P. Jamieson, Wendy Berry Mendes, and Matthew K. Nock, "Improving Acute Stress Responses: The Power of Reappraisal," *Current Directions of Psychological Science* 22, no. 51 (2013): 53, doi: 10.1177/0963721412461500.

8. Abiola Keller et al., "Does the Perception That Stress Affects Health Matter? The Association with Health and Mortality," *Health Psychology* 31, no. 5 (2012): 677, doi: 10.1037/a0026743.

9. Marcus Buckingham, *The One Thing You Need to Know . . . About Great Managing, Great Leading, and Sustained Individual Success* (New York: Free Press, 2005), 5.

10. Ibid., 120–25.

INDEX

accuracy, 19; disregard of, 7
affect, 27, 32, 88, 117n1
amusement, 27
anger, ix, 39, 41
annoyance, 12, 14, 39, 92
anxiety, ix, 27; arousal, and, 45–47;
 avoidance of, 7; blended nature of,
 39–42; cognitive reappraisal of, 45;
 definition of, 36; excessive levels of,
 35; fear and, 38–39; as a friend, 35;
 history of, 36–38; neurotic, 37;
 realistic, 37; reappraisal of, 99–100;
 responding to, 42–44, 44–45; signal,
 37; self-medicating and, 7. *See also*
 attention; fear
appraisal system, 32–33
arousal: procrastinating as, 46; optimal
 levels of, 45–46
attention, 29; affect-biased, 29; anxiety,
 and, 44; magnification of emotion,
 and, 31
awe, 27

biologically based emotion, 25–28;
 intensity and presentation of, 26
Bois, J. Samuel, 77–78
Buckingham, Marcus, 103

cognition, 1, 31–32; attitude change, and,
 32
compassion, 27

conscientiousness, 19, 71–73
culture, 2, 5, 30, 34, 39, 42, 51;
 acceptability of emotional expression,
 and, 30, 42. *See also* scripts

daydream, 7
deadline: absolute, 15, 16, 17; creation of,
 95; extension fantasies, 16–17, 59, 102,
 107; requiring, 106–107
deadline-driven, 5, 19–20, 21, 22, 23, 41,
 43, 46, 57, 65, 66, 68, 71, 73, 74, 76,
 78, 79, 81, 84, 85, 86, 90, 94, 96, 97,
 98, 101, 104, 106–108, 114, 116,
 118n1, 119n12, 122n20; definition of,
 4; illustration of, 7–9; urgency, 28. *See
 also* procrastination
decision making, 2, 13
depression, 2, 59
disgust, 28, 39, 40, 112; anxiety, 41;
 combined with distress, 39
distraction, 8, 19, 21–23, 44, 100, 103
distress, ix, 3, 112; anxiety, and, 39–41;
 shame, and, 55

Ekman, Paul, 27
embarrassment, 27, 112
emotion, 1–9, 25–34; amplification of, 37,
 40; blending of, 27, 38, 41; disruption
 from, 97–99; energizing quality of,
 46–47; ideology, fueled by, 114;
 images of failure, and, 50; independent

ABOUT THE AUTHOR

Mary Lamia, PhD, is a clinical psychologist and psychoanalyst who practices in Marin County, California. Additionally, she is a professor and faculty chair at the Wright Institute in Berkeley. Her career-long passion for conveying an understanding of emotions to the public is exemplified by her writing and media work. She is the author of *Emotions! Making Sense of Your Feelings* and *Understanding Myself: A Kid's Guide to Intense Emotions and Strong Feelings*. She coauthored *The White Knight Syndrome: Rescuing Yourself from Your Need to Rescue Others* and a forthcoming book, *The Upside of Shame*. She has provided numerous television, radio, Internet, and print media interviews, and for nearly a decade she has hosted a weekly call-in talk show, *KidTalk with Dr. Mary*, on Radio Disney stations. Her blog posts for *Psychology Today* and *Therapy Today* illustrate the significant role of emotions in our lives.

.